YOUR KNOWLEDGE HAS

Bibliographic information published by the German National Library:

The German National Library lists this publication in the National Bibliography; detailed bibliographic data are available on the Internet at http://dnb.dnb.de .

Imprint:

Copyright © 2017 GRIN Verlag
Print and binding: Books on Demand GmbH, Norderstedt Germany
ISBN: 9783668943407

Aasia Rehman

Detection of Primary User Emulation Attack in Cognitive Radio Networks based on TDOA using Novel Bat Algorithm

GRIN Verlag

GRIN - Your knowledge has value

Since its foundation in 1998, GRIN has specialized in publishing academic texts by students, college teachers and other academics as e-book and printed book. The website www.grin.com is an ideal platform for presenting term papers, final papers, scientific essays, dissertations and specialist books.

Detection of Primary User Emulation Attack in Cognitive Radio Networks Based On TDOA Using Novel Bat Algorithm

Dissertation Submitted to
Shri Mata Vaishno Devi University

For the Award of the degree of

Master of Technology
in
Computer Science and Engineering

Submitted by
Aasia Rehman

Department of Computer Science and Engineering
SHRI MATA VAISHNO DEVI UNIVERSITY
Kakryal, Katra - 182320, J&K(India)
May, 2017

ACKNOWLEDGEMENT

The satisfaction that accompanies the successful completion of any tasks would be incomplete without the mention of the people who made it possible and whose encouragement and guidance has been a source of inspiration throughout the course of this work.

I thank Almighty Allah for His kind blessings which helped me to complete this thesis.

I owe my sincere gratitude to my project supervisor Mr. Deo Prakash, for his constructive suggestions, scholastic guidance, constant inspiration, valuable advices and kind co-operation for the successful completion of this work.

I express my profound gratitude to my colleagues and all my friends for their useful discussions and support.

I would also like to thank my parents for their constant support and blessings, who are my inspiration and pillars of strength.

Aasia Rehman
Entry No. 15MMS004
SMVD University, Katra
May 2017

ABSTRACT

Cognitive Radio Network (CRN) Technology makes the efficient utilization of scarce spectrum resources by allowing the unlicensed users to opportunistically use the licensed spectrum bands. Cognitive Radio Technology has gained a lot of attention from the researchers over the years however insufficient research has been done related to its security. Cognitive Radio Network due to its flexible and open nature is vulnerable to a number of security attacks. In this thesis we recognize different types of attacks at different layers of protocol stack. This thesis is mainly concerned with one of the physical layer attack called Primary User Emulation Attack and its detection. PUE Attack adversely affects the CRN performance and can also sometimes lead to Denial of Service to CR networks. In Primary User Emulation Attack the attacker imitates the signal characteristics of the Primary User. This thesis first provides introduction to CRN, its architecture and sensing techniques and also discusses various attacks and their counter measures. Then it mainly focuses on PUE attack and examines its mitigation techniques. This thesis solves the problem of PUE attack by localization technique based on TDOA measurements with reduced error in location estimation using a Novel Bat Algorithm (NBA). A number of cooperative secondary users are used for detecting the PUEA by comparing its estimated position with the known position of incumbent. The main goal of Novel Bat Algorithm (NBA) is to minimize two fitness functions namely non-linear least square (NLS) and the maximum likelihood (ML) in order to optimize the error in estimation. After evaluation, simulation results clearly demonstrates that NBA results in reduced estimation error as compared to Taylor Series Estimation (TSE) and Particle Swarm Optimization (PSO) and it also needs smaller number of secondary users for cooperation. Also maximum likelihood function performs better than non-linear least square function.

TABLE OF CONTENTS

LIST OF FIGURES

LIST OF TABLES

LIST OF ABBREVIATIONS

CR	Cognitive Radio
CRN	Cognitive Radio Networks
PU	Primary User
SU	Secondary User
FCC	Federal Communication Commission
SDR	Software Defined Radio
DSA	Dynamic Spectrum Access
PUE	Primary User Emulation
SSDF	Spectrum Sensing Data Falsification
CCSD	Control Channel Saturation DoS
SCN	Selfish Channel Negotiation
SNR	Signal to Noise Ratio
TDOA	Time Difference of Arrival
TOA	Time of Arrival
RSS	Received Signal Strength
WSN	Wireless Sensor Networks
BS	Base-Station
NBA	Novel Bat Algorithm
PSO	Particle Swarm Optimization
TSE	Taylor Series Estimation
GWO	Grey Wolf Optimizer

Chapter 1

INTRODUCTION TO COGNITIVE RADIO NETWORKS

1.1 Introduction

A lot of research studies have shown that most of the licensed spectrum is not utilized sufficiently in temporal as well as spatial spheres. The white spaces in the licensed spectrum present considerably high opportunity for a number of wireless applications. Thus cognitive radio network technology has been developed to utilize this opportunity. In cognitive radio networks secondary users or Cognitive Radios dynamically senses for white spaces in the licensed band using spectrum sensing algorithms and uses them for communication purposes. In other words Cognitive Radio in CRN is a radio that senses the spectrum band for free channels and then adapts its transmitting parameters (modulation type, frame size, operating frequency, transmitting power etc.) according to the environment to allow concurrent wireless communication through the same frequency band [1]. We have two different types of cognitive radio nodes: the policy radios and the learning radios [2].

• Policy Radios detect the behavior of the cognitive radio by analyzing some predefined policies. When the environment is sensed, the radio collects the data from the environment and then extracts useful information from it which we called statistics which in turn gives the state of the radio.

• Learning Radios in addition have a learning engine that is used to arrange and rearrange the states of the radios.

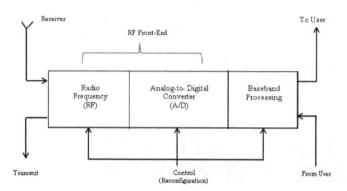

Figure 1.1: CR Transceiver

To distinguish CR from the traditional radios, CR has novel radio frequency transceiver architecture [3]. The important parts of transceiver are as shown in the figure 1.1 [4] the RF front end which consists of Radio Frequency and Analog-to-Digital converter, and a Baseband processing. Both the parts are reconfigured through a control bus to readjust according to the changing RF-environment. The received signal is amplified, mixed and analog-to-digital converted in the RF front end unit. Next the signal is modulated or demodulated and encoded or decoded in the Baseband processing unit. The most important feature of the CR transceiver is the ability of the RF front end to perform wideband sensing. This ability of RF front end is mainly concerned with the RF hardware technologies e.g. wideband antenna, power amplifier, Mixer, Voltage-controlled oscillator (VCO) and adaptive filter. RF hardware should be able to tune to any portion of the spectrum band.

Cognitive Radio networks: CRN network is formed by putting together several CRs (unlicensed users) to construct a network together with the legitimate users of the spectrum band. The cognitive radio in CRN is a device that first senses the surroundings i.e. environment and then trains from it and reconfigure its internal framework as per the data that is sensed. It has two main goals robust communication anywhere and anytime and valuable use of the available frequency spectrum.

The term Cognitive Radio was first introduced by Mitola in 2000 as an extension to software defined radio (SDR) [5]. The primary intension was to efficiently utilize the spectrum band. With the increase in the number of

---

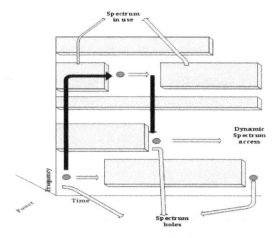

Figure 1.2: Dynamic Spectrum Access

wireless networks in the internet the need for spectrum also increases rapidly and hence there is the scarcity of frequency bands for these networks or applications. The main idea was to develop an intelligent agent embedded in lightweight equipments like PDAs to accomplish the basic transmission requirements of the user. Use of vacant frequency bands or vacant channels in the spectrum band anywhere anytime is referred to as Dynamic Spectrum Access (DSA) [6] as shown in fig. 1.2 [3][1]. As a result of this the Federal Communications Commission (FCC) allowed the use of certified spectrum by the prohibited users. Thus the unlicensed users can utilize the free spectrum but it should not intervene with the primary users. The problem of spectrum shortage was reduced due to the cognitive radio technology.

1.1.1 Working Process of CRN

A CRN have four main working functionalities as shown in figure 1.3:
1. Cognitive Ability
2. Self-concerned Ability
3. Decision capability
4. Re-configurable capability

1. Cognitive Ability [5]: The CR networks have the ability of sensing the spectrum and determine if there are any spectrum holes available in the

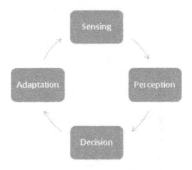

Figure 1.3: working process of CR

network. If the spectrum holes are detected then the unauthorized users uses that band for communication causing less intrusion for licensed users. Various algorithms are used for sensing the spectrum. The CR also enables spectrum sharing, location recognition, network detection and service detection.

2. Self-organize Ability [5]: A CR in CRN should collaborate and self-organize so as to produce efficient performance of the network by allowing the operation of only those CR nodes which are needed while disabling those nodes which are not needed for communication.

3. Decision capability [5]: The CRN needs to decide on the use of resources that are shared, a modification in parameters and nodes configuration etc.

4. Re-configurable capability [5]: There are various re-configurable abilities of CRN's some of them are as: Frequency agility, Dynamic frequency selection, Adaptive modulation, Power change, Access to dynamic networks.

1.1.2 CRN Architecture

There are 3 prime architectures of CRNs [5]. The elementary parts of each of the architectures are Base Stations, Mobile stations and the backbone architecture [5]. These 3 architectures are as under:

1. Infrastructure architecture: In infrastructure architecture as shown in figure 1.4 each mobile station are able to contact with other mobile station only if both of them are under the area of same base station. The services of each CR are explained in advance in this type of architecture. It is centralized architecture with a central base station. The data collected by every CR device is transferred towards the prime base station.

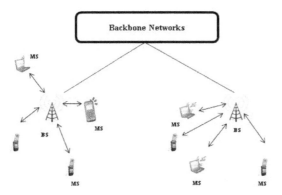

Figure 1.4: Infrastructure Architecture

2. Ad hoc architecture: Ad hoc has no backbone network base as shown in figure 1.5. The mobile station watches its environment to detect if there are few mobile stations that can be connected by using protocols then they are joined by a communication link thus it forms ad hoc architecture. Thus the nodes are linked via an ad hoc contact on both authorized and unauthorized frequency bands. In this type each CR node has all the abilities and can predict the next level in an affair using the local information that it obtained during observation. This local information is not ample for determining the effect of its behavior on the network due to which co-operative techniques are useful where this locally observed information is shared with other nodes to widen the capability of the whole CR network.

3. Mesh architecture: The Mesh architecture is a mix of both infrastructure as well as ad hoc architecture as shown in figure 1.6. The Base station is linked to others through wireless connections. They form the basis for the mesh architecture. Mobile stations are joined to base station either directly or via several mobile stations. It has the supremacy and limitations of both the architectures.

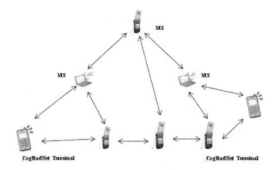

Figure 1.5: Adhoc Architecture

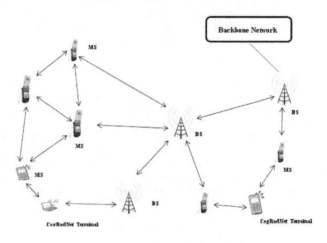

Figure 1.6: Mesh Architecture

1.2 CRN Functions And Their Challenges

The various functions performed by cognitive radio network and their challenges are as under:

1. Spectrum sensing: Sensing the spectrum is necessary requisite for making CRN realistic. A CR node should know about the modification in its environment [5]. Spectrum sensing makes cognitive radios to reconfigure themselves as per the surrounding by identifying the band holes not causing any disturbance to licensed users.

Few challenges of sensing the spectrum are as under:

• Measurement of Interference: A CR does not completely know the position of primary receivers due to the weak inter-communication among primary users and CRs. Therefore modern methods are needed to determine the interference measurement at the primary networks [5].

• Multi-user network spectrum sensing: In case of multiple secondary users and primary users it becomes more complex to sense the bands and measure interference. Thus new efficient procedures need to be built for band sensing in case of multi user networks [5].

• Efficient spectrum sensing: The cognitive radio is not able to implement both sensing and transmit data simultaneously. It is known as sensing efficiency problem. As a result transmitting should not take place while sensing the spectrum. Also specific algorithms must be developed so that the time to sense the spectrum should be reduced under the sensing preciseness [5].

• Covered Primary user problem: Here CR users affect the licensed users because the primary signal cannot be identified due to its position [5].

2. Decision about spectrum: Once the spectrum has been sensed CRN requires deciding among various spectrum bands that are available, which one is most suitable one to be used for communication based on quality of service specific to the function.

Challenges:

• Reconfigure: The methods of cognitive radio networks reconfigures the certain features of transportation for the ideal performance in a specific spectrum [5].

• Decision of spectrum band between dissimilar bands: A CRN needs to perform spectrum selection process in authorized as well as unauthorized spectrum [5].

3. Sharing Of Spectrum: Sharing spectrum involves 2 categories: sharing within the same cognitive radio network and sharing between different cognitive radio networks.

Challenges:

• CCC (common control channel): CCC is useful in sharing of spectrum performance. However its application is impractical for the reason that it should be relinquished at any time when the primary user selects it [5].

• Dynamic Radio range: The operational frequency of CRs is usually modified due to dependency among operational frequency and range of radio. Till now no task has been done to overcome this problem [5].

• Knowledge of Position: Unauthorized users are constantly instructed about the licensed users position and energy. This knowledge about the primary users position is used to validate every user in order to give security and authentication in networks [5].

4. Mobility of spectrum: The mobility of spectrum means frequency hand off when a PU becomes active in the licensed band which is occupied by the secondary users then the secondary user needs to move from one spectrum to another that is not used. This step is to ensure the stable interaction at the time of hand off of spectrum bands.

Challenges:

• Time domain mobility: Based on the possibility of unused spectrum bands CRN adapts to the band. Due to the changing nature of the unused spectrum bands the quality of service here has turn out to be a threat [5].

• Space mobility: As the secondary users shift from point to point over time the presence of accessible bands also switches over time. Thus regular allotment of unused bands in these networks is a challenging problem [5].

1.3   Cognitive Radio Engine Architecture

Cognitive radio consists of 4 main parts as shown in figure 1.7: Software defined radio, knowledge base, reasoning engine, learning engine [7]. SDR is a device that can be highly configured. It has leading end that can be adjusted to different frequencies and it also has an amplifier which permits interaction at various levels of power. A modem can apply different modulation techniques. It also has a number of input sensors that can accept digital RF input and provide significant outcomes. E.g. an energy detector can calculate the power that is received at a certain frequency to indicate if the band is already in use or not. There are also number of receiver sensors that can be used to figure out signal to noise ratio, bit error rate and frame error rate. The SDR interface introduces these input and output sets to a controlling entity which chooses a collection of inputs and produces a set of optimal outputs which is defined by objective function. Inputs are chosen by an optimization problem which is handled by cognitive engine. The inputs are given to the engines, knowledge base as read-only data or read-write

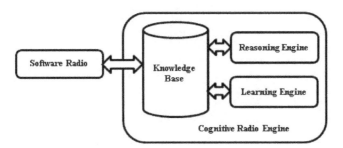

Figure 1.7: CRN Engine Architecture

data. The knowledge base consists of a collection of intelligent explanations that denotes the radios state. The cognitive engine consists of two engines the reasoning and the learning engine. Reasoning engine is present in both policy radios and learning radio whereas learning engine is present only in learning radio. There are reasoning rules in the reasoning engine to which a collection of actions, circumstances in which these action are executed, and also by virtue of what the state of knowledge base is affected by these actions. In case of learning radios the learning engine tries all possible configurations in order to view how the CR reacts to them. They use algorithms like AI, search, neural networks and evolutionary. A cognitive radio works on the basis of a cognitive cycle as Observe, orient, plan, decide and act and incase of learning radio extra step is added i.e. learn [8]. In attacking the CRs the intruder needs to operate on observe step and rest will be affected automatically.

1.4 Spectrum Sensing

Spectrum sensing is one of the essential tasks of a CR node. The primary objective of spectrum sensing is to identify the holes in the spectrum and primary users in licensed spectrum band. A CR node senses the surrounding environment for the availability of the spectrum holes in the particular frequency band then utilizes these spectrum holes for the efficient communication and also leaves the spectrum immediately whenever a PU is identified so that no obstruction is caused to primary system. The most important challenging issue for CR node in spectrum sensing is making sure that the sensing results are error free, that may occur due to the hidden node problem. This issue is removed to some extent in distributed spectrum sensing; where every CR node performs the local spectrum sensing and sends the sensed outcome to the data collector which with the help of several methods produces the final results of sensing. Spectrum sensing techniques are grouped into 3 classes as [9] shown in figure 1.8: Non-cooperative sensing, Cooperative sensing, Interference sensing.

• Non-cooperative sensing: It is also known as transmitter detection technique [9]. It is further divided as energy detection [15], matched filter detection and Cyclo-stationary feature methods [15]. In energy detection primary user is sensed according to detected energy. This is the easiest method and it does not depend on any previous data of PU system. Energy detection is the most widely used method for spectrum sensing [10] [11]. In this method the energy of the entering signal is co-related with a predetermined threshold to detect the primary signal. The matched filter method decides the existence of licensed users by analyzing the signal to noise ratio. The fundamental limitation of the matched filter is that it depends upon the prior awareness of the primary system signal features. Cyclo-stationary feature detection method works by detecting the existence of primary system by analyzing the low signal to noise ratio. Cyclo-Stationary is the most complex method. It also needs former awareness of the primary signal. Here the signal is first sampled and then its amplitude is normalized. The peak value of amplitude is compared with the predefined threshold if periodicity is detected then the band is occupied by the primary signal. Otherwise band is free to be used.

• Cooperative Sensing: It is also divided into 3 categories [9] Centralized Coordinated, Decentralized Coordinated and Decentralized Uncoordinated [12] [13]. In centralized Coordinated, a CR node performs sensing to reveal the existence of primary transmitter or receiver and sends the sensed data to the central entity which in turn broadcasts the message to each and every CR node. In Decentralized Coordinated, there is no need of centralized entity in the network. In Decentralized un-coordinated method every CR node performs sensing independent of the other and leaves the band if a primary user is sensed but does not inform the other CR nodes about it.

• Interference Detection: It consists of 2 categories Interference temperature management and primary receiver detection [9]. In interference temperature management an upper bound of an interference limit is initialized for the spectrum band in a particular geographic location not permitting the CR nodes to cause hindrance using the particular band in a particular location.Its main goal is to calculate interference at the receiver. In primary receiver detection an inexpensive sensor is placed in the close vicinity of primary receiver to sense the power released by it so that it can be detected.

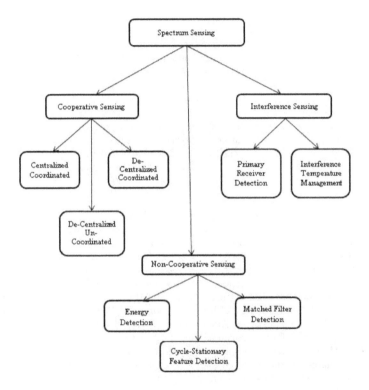

Figure 1.8: Spectrum Sensing Techniques

The sensor later sends the collected data to the cognitive radio nodes to know the spectrum availability [9].

1.5 Objective of the Thesis

The main objective of my thesis is as follows:
• To study the various Attacks in Cognitive Radio Networks and their Counter measures.
• To detect the Primary User Emulation Attack in Cognitive Radio Networks using the localization technique based on TDOA measurements in combination with optimization algorithm known as Novel Bat Algorithm in order to enhance the performance of detection technique by optimizing the mean error in estimating the location of attacker.
• To evaluate performance of Novel Bat Algorithm by optimizing two cost functions that is Non-Linear least square cost function and maximum likelihood cost function and compare it with the Particle Swarm Optimization and Taylor Series Estimation. In addition to this, to compare the performance of Grey Wolf Optimizer with the Particle Swarm Optimization.

1.6 Organization of the Thesis

The remainder of the thesis is organized as follows: In Chapter 2, Security Requisites for CRN, Attacks like Primary User Emulation Attack, Objective Function Attack, Jamming, Overlapping Secondary Nodes, Spectrum Sensing Data Falsification Attack, Control Channel Saturation DoS Attack, Selfish Channel Negotiation (SCN), Sinkhole Attack, Hello Flood Attack, Sybil Attack, Wormhole Attack, Key-Depletion Attack, Cognitive Radio virus, Lion Attack and Jellyfish Attack and their counter measures are discussed.
In Chapter 3, Literature Survey about Primary User Emulation Attack and its Mitigation techniques are discussed in detail.
In Chapter 4, the proposed system for detection of primary user emulation attack, mathematical model for the system, Novel Bat Algorithm and Particle Swarm Optimization are discussed.
In Chapter 5, Simulation results are analysed. Chapter 6, Concludes the thesis and future scope is discussed.

Chapter 2

SECURITY IN COGNITIVE RADIO NETWORKS

2.1 Security In CRN

CRNs are flexible and unprotected as compared to conventional networks so they are more susceptible to security threats. The simplest of attack is, if the results of cognitive sensing are changed by a malicious user as a result normal functioning of the network will be disturbed. There are 3 main security needs as confidentiality, integrity and availability in CRNs [5].

2.1.1 Security Requisites for CRN

CRNs are more sensitive to security attacks relative to other wireless communication networks because of its inherent nature. Some of the security requisites for CRNs are as under [5]:
• Data Integrity: Data integrity is the fundamental security component in case of wireless networks as compared to networks that uses wires because WLANs are affected by burglars users easily. Data integrity guards the data from modification that is being transferred; there is no inserting of data or deleting of data etc.
• Data Confidentiality: Data confidentiality makes certain that the data that is being transferred is not readable to malicious users.
• Authentication: Authentication makes sure that the unlicensed users cannot approach to sensitive data. In CRNs Authentication is considered as one of the elemental security requisite for CRNs because in CRN we need to

differentiate secondary users from primary users.

• Identification: Identification is defined as a procedure in which each user is given a name or identification number. In CRN each secondary user has identification method in it. Detecting the services and identifying the SUs are the fundamental components for building the adequate and authentic CRN.

• Availability: Availability is a process where authorized and non-authorized users are allowed to utilize the frequency spectrum in CRNs. In case of authorized or primary users, it means using the accessible band to transfer data and not being intervened by secondary users and in case of secondary user it means using the accessible holes of the spectrum band to transfer data and not causing any disturbance to licensed users of that band. This component helps to prohibit DoS outbreaks.

• Non-repudiation: Non repudiation prohibits the transmitter or receiver from refusing the transferred data. The non-repudiation method is useful to validate the misdeed and restrict the invader from the network if an invader is recognized as disobeying the rules.

2.2 CRN Security Attacks And Defense Methods

The different security attacks on CRNs can be classified as: The physical layer attacks, the MAC layer attacks, the transport layer attacks, application layer attacks and cross layer attacks. The physical layer attacks are Primary User Emulation Attack, Objective function attack, jamming, overlapping secondary nodes. The data link layer attacks are Spectrum Sensing Data Falsification, Control Channel Saturation DoS Attack, and Selfish Channel Negotiation. The network layer attacks are HELLO flood attacks, sinkhole attacks, Sybil attack and wormhole attack. The transport layer attack is Key Depletion attack. Application layer attack includes cognitive radio viruses and cross layer attacks include lion attack and jellyfish attack. We have two main security outbreaks the selfish attack and the malicious attacks.

• Selfish attacks: Here the mischievous user urges to utilize the band with great preference. It gives the other unauthorized users confidence that it is the authorized user of the band. Due to this the selfish user occupies the band as much as he wishes [14].

• Malicious attacks: In this the invader does not allow the other user to use the band creating the Denial of Service (DoS) [14].

The various attacks on CRN are as follows:

2.2.1 Physical Layer Attacks:

Physical layer is the first layer of protocol stack which acts as an interface to the data communication medium. It includes everything that is required for communication between two network nodes like optical fiber, network interface card etc. and in case of CRN we can say the environment. The various attacks that target the physical layer and their defense methods are as under and in table 2.1:

2.2.1.1 Primary User Emulation Attack

In PUE outbreak the mischievous unauthorized user imitates or acts as a licensed system to use the available spectrum without sharing the spectrum with other CR secondary nodes. The main motive of this attack is categorized into selfish attack and malicious attack. The PUE affects each type of radios, the policy radio and the learning radio with various austerities. In case of policy radio as early as the intruder frees the band the aftermath of the outbreak disappears. The CR users then realize that the band is free and uses it. In case of learning radios the present and prior knowledge about licensed users is collected and the time of leaving the band is determined from it. When the spectrum is freed the intruder executes this attack and will last for a longer time. Various types of PUE attacks can take place having the little information of CRNs.

• Defense Mechanisms: For defending the PUE outbreak we need to detect the identification of the node that transmits the signals or data whether it is a licensed system or a mischievous user. However the defense methods should not make any alteration in the primary system according to FCC rules.

i. Cryptographic mechanism for authentication: e.g. digital signatures, but it has a disadvantage that it requires the modification of primary user which is not allowed by FCC protocols.

ii. Distance Ratio Test (DRT) and Distance Difference Test (DDT) [16]: DRT depends on determining the power of signal that is received and DDT depends on inequality in phases of signal. Both of them use the transmitter verification procedure. Both depends on trusted location verifiers LVs (master LVs and slave LVs). The disadvantage of DDT is that a compact synchronization is required between LVs and both of them can be deceived if the attacker is nearest to the tower.

iii. Loc-Def: In LocDef sender is verified in 3 steps: validating the signal features, analyzing the strength of received signal and localization of source. It gathers the Radio Spectrum Sensing measurements using WSN to recognize the position of sender [17].

iv. Time Difference of Arrival (TDOA) and Frequency Difference of Arrival (FDOA): It first applies TDOA and then TDOA provides some inputs to FDOA which determines the correct position of the sender [18]. It has a limitation that it is based on various hypotheses as a result it cannot be applied to CRNs.

v. Fingerprinting [19]: It authenticates the sender. Earlier RF fingerprinting was used which identifies the sender as the emitter in the waveforms. This approach is complex although it gives an optimum explanation so a new method called cross layer pattern recognition was defined to defeat this disadvantage. It uses the features of electromagnetic signatures in nodes to develop a secure system.

2.2.1.2 Objective Function Attack

The cognitive radio is authoritative to modify various features which include frequency, bandwidth, power, modulation type, coding rate encryption type and frame size to satisfy certain criteria like less consumption of power, high data rate, and high security and each has its own weight depending on the specific operation. Cognitive radio operates on one or more features so as to reach the goal as close as possible. One or more objective functions are interpreted to achieve various features for the CR node. When cognitive radio interprets the objective function to determine the nodes features the malicious user can operate on the features which it can supervise (transfer rate) that disturbs the final results.

For example in case of emails high security and low power may be needed while for videos high data rate and high security may be needed.

We consider an objective function as under [7]:

$F = w_1 P + w_2 R + w_3 S$

Here w_1, w_2, w_3 are the weights associated with power, rate and security respectively.

For example a CR wants to use security level of s_2 but the malicious user makes it to use a lower level of s_1 i.e. $s_1 < s_2$. If the user wishes to use s_2 the malicious user creates a jam in the band by reducing the R from r_2 to r_1 where $r_2 > r_1$ due to which the final objective function is decreased. As a result the malicious user enforces the CR user to implement lower security so that it can be easily breached.

• Defense Mechanism: Simplest mechanism [20] is to use threshold values for the radio parameters and if the parameters do not satisfy the thresholds the interaction is halted. Its limitation is that it depends on fixed thresholds. Another method is to use good IDS. In [21][22] the authors proposed a covert adaptive injection attack. As an example of objective function attack the

Table 2.1: Physical Layer Attacks and Counter Measures

S. No.	Type Of Attack	Counter Measure
1.	PUE	i) DRT-depending on SS measures ii) DDT- depending on signal phase difference iii) LocDef- depending on location of transmitters iv) TDOA & FDOA v) Fingerprinting
2.	Objective Function attack	i) Assign a threshold value to each and every CR parameter if the parameter does not satisfy the threshold value then interaction halts. ii) Method based on local thresholds iii) Neighborhood voting system
3.	Jamming	i) Create a statistical framework to define the difference among natural and unnatural levels of noise ii) Comparison between SS and PDR-if SS is large and PDR is small the node is blocked if one of the neighboring nodes do not have large SS and PDR iii) Location Consistency checks iv) Frequency Hopping
4.	Overlapping Secondary nodes	i) Modulation scheme modification ii) Detection and Avoidance of attacks iii) Adopting authentication and trust model

malicious node is able to learn and modify its parameters according to the changing atmosphere. Here the malicious node attempts to secretly modify the sensing results of the distributed CRN, disrupting the objective function. A powerful distributed outlier detection technique is proposed to mitigate the covert adaptive injection attack. In [22] the authors used local thresholds at each device. Thus it becomes very difficult for the intruder to assume the thresholds of all the neighboring devices at any moment. If an attacker is detected by the device it transmits a primitive alarm to its one hop neighbors. If a device receives the primitive alarms from more than half of the devices which are common neighbors of the device and the malicious device, the alarm is not dispatched rather it is broadcasted as a confirmed alarm. The attacker is validated by using hash based calculations. In [21] the authors proposed a neighborhood voting system. Here each device after receiving the sensing data from their one hop neighbors compute algorithm based mean and performs a spatial correlation test. Every device casts a vote regarding the validity of its neighbors depending on the results. The device is declared as an attacker if more than half of neighbors vote suspects it as the attacker.

2.2.1.3 Jamming

In jamming the intruder can transmit data packets continuously that block the other participants of the communication to transmit or receive the data. The jammer continuously sends the data packets as a result of which the authorized user can never ever sense the channel as free or it may send the packets to the user and convince them to accept trash packets. In addition jammers are also able to disturb the interaction among users by destroying the packets in transit. More threatening effect of a jammer is that it disrupts the communication link between cognitive nodes that they use to interchange the spectrum sensing results. This type of outbreak takes place in both physical and MAC layers. There are mainly 4 categories of jammers [23] as Constant Jammer which transmits the packets in continuity without waiting for the band to be free, Deceptive jammer fools the authorized users and transmits the packet towards them in continuity causing the users to shift to receiving mode, Random jammer which sends the packets in intervals i.e. it waits between the transmission of packets and at last reactive jammer which continuously watches over the band and whenever it observes interaction is taking place in the channel it sends the jamming packets. For layer 1 of OSI jamming, the intruder uses equipment that generates the energy having equal frequency used by the users to interact causing disturbance. For MAC layer jamming, the intruder transmits the packets over a specific frequency band causing other users to think that the band is busy thus, delaying their communication.

• Defense Mechanism: As jamming takes place in both physical and MAC layer so it should be defended on both layers. In case of MAC layer revelation the users can determine the occurrence of outbreak by watching the band continuously using the CSMA protocol of MAC layer. In CSMA the channel is watched till it is found to be free and even after it is found free the user still waits for an arbitrary time after that it uses the channel. The CSMA will never sense the channel to be free in case the band is already in use or used by the intruder so the user backs off the communication. In case of physical layer CR nodes must be capable of detecting the abnormality in the noise level of the channels [24]. This is done by gathering the information about the noise levels in the whole network then developing a systematic model for performing the comparison when DoS attack occurs. A technique of studying the relationship between the signal strength (SS) and packet delivery ratio (PDR) is used for jamming detection [23]. If SS is large and PDR is less the authorized user considers that jamming has occurred. This technique is called signal strength consistency checks. Other technique is the location consistency checks. Here the position of neighbors is important that can be obtained through GPS and broadcasted by every node but GPS may not always exist in CRN. The nodes neighbors must have large PDR but if the neighbors have small PDR then the node is considered to be under jamming attack. Frequency hopping is a good defense technique where the participants use different channel to communicate if DoS attack takes place. Spatial retreat is a method where the participant alters its location to leave the interference range.

2.2.1.4 Overlapping Secondary Nodes

The Dynamic Spectrum access sharing may be under threat when more than one secondary network overlap and coexist in the same geographical area either through incumbent vulnerabilities or through objective function, carried out by a malicious user or randomly by a loyal user [26][6]. Signals emitted by the malicious node in one network can affect adversely to incumbent and secondary nodes of both the networks. These emitted signals may deliver erroneous sensing data which may affect the objective function adversely in both the networks. These malicious nodes may even wrongly imitate the incumbents of both the networks periodically causing the networks to free the occupied bands. In addition to this in some cases a loyal user while declaring the appearance of incumbent in first network may recklessly deliver the similar data to the 2nd network which affects the objective function of 2nd network adversely.

- Defense Method: This type of attack is difficult to mitigate because the secondary nodes of the targeted network do not have explicit control over the malicious users. This type of attack originally attacks the abilities of the CR network for performing spectrum sensing and sharing of infrastructure and Adhoc networks which is a DoS. In [25] the authors proposed three schemes for defending this type of attack which are also suitable for various other DoS attacks. The three schemes are as under:

1. Modulation scheme modification [26]: The influence of DoS attacks can be reduced by using frequency hopping and direct spread spectrum methods. However they may still be able to reduce the QoS (Quality of Service).

2. Detection and Avoidance of attacks [26]: A malicious user can be recognized by the network, by analyzing the incumbents position and features of the transmitted signal.

3. Adopting authentication and trust model [26]: The authors in the paper [27] developed a system to calculate certain values like trust value, suspicion level and consistency level to recognize and eliminate the malicious node. For each user trust value is determined over time while as consistency level determines the consistent trust level over time and the users become suspicious if the state of channel delivered by it does not match with the state of channel delivered by remaining users. A user will be identified as malicious and will be eliminated from the network if its trust value is consistently low.

2.2.2 MAC layer attacks

MAC (Medium Access Control) layer is a sub-part of the data link layer which is developed to allow the medium to be shared among multiple nodes in the same network. To regulate the users access Common Control Channel is used to interchange control messages. The various attacks that target MAC layer and their defense methods are as follows and shown in table 2.2:

2.2.2.1 Spectrum Sensing Data Falsification (SSDF)

This type is also called Byzantine Attack. Here the malicious user sends the wrong sensing outcomes gathered locally either to a node or to the information gathering center due to which the node or the gathering center gives the inaccurate final verdict [28][29]. It takes place in both centralized and distributed CRNs but the attack is more dangerous for the distributed CRNs. In case of centralized, whole of the data is forwarded to the gathering center which then decides which of the bands are free and which are busy. Tricking the center may either disallow the authorized users to utilize the band or it grants permission to the user to utilize the band that is formally busy thus

Table 2.2: MAC Layer Attacks and Counter Measures

S.no	Type of attack	Counter-Measure
1.	SSDF	i) Fusion method in which entire sensing results are added up and then related to threshold to disclose the outbreak. ii) Weighted sequential ratio test. iii) Weight based fusion method. iv) Method that need previous information. v) Neyman-Pearson Test
2.	CCSD	Trust based method
3.	SCN	Trust based method

effecting the communication. Same procedure is done in distributed networks but here spectrum verdicts are made cooperatively by cognitive radio nodes.

• Detection and Defense Mechanism:

i. Decision fusion technique [30]: Here the entire spectrum sensing result gathered locally is added up and if the addition result is > or = to a certain threshold then it determines that the band is engaged with the primary user else it is free. The limitation of Decision fusion method is that rising or reducing the threshold has great effect on the decision.

ii. Weighted sequential ratio test [31]: This test is used to defend the SSDF outbreak. It has 2 steps first is reputation maintenance step and second is the hypotheses test step. At first every node has a reputation value of 0 which is increased by 1 upon each correct sensing report. The hypotheses step depends on sequential probability ratio test.

iii. Weight based fusion scheme [32]: This is also a defending method. Here a trust approach and pre-filtering methods are used. Invaders are of 2 categories Always yes which reveals the existence of primary system and Always no that detects that the primary system is absent. It is based on pre-filtering method to detect and invalidate the intruders which are occasionally invalid and not invalid and giving every CR node a trust aspect which immediately reveals the Always yes and Always no devices.

iv. Detection Mechanism [33]: It compares the local spectrum sensing result with the global result in the fusion center over a time period. It only works when fusion center is available.

v. Bayesian detection mechanism [34]: Here former awareness about the local spectrum sensing results should be known. Its limitation is that when CRN is under SSDF attack former awareness is not authentic and thus this solution is no longer the optimal solution.

vi. Ney-man Pearson test [35]: It does not require the former awareness of final spectrum result but it requires the former awareness probabilities of local sensing. It operates by defining either the largest tolerable probability of fake alarm or largest tolerable probability of omitted detection.

2.2.2.2 Control channel saturation DoS attack

This type of attack takes place in multi-hop CRNs. In multi-hop CRN, CR nodes interact with one another by compromising the spectrum band in a shared aspect. In this process medium access control frames are interchanged between nodes to get the spectrum band allotted to them. When more number of nodes desire to interact at the same time the CCC is saturated as it can handle only a limited number of simultaneous access to the spectrum band. The malicious user can exploit this characteristic and can produce spurious medium access control frames to saturate the band and as a result network performance decreases drastically to about zero throughput.

2.2.2.3 Selfish Channel Negotiation (SCN)

In multi-hop CRN, a CR node may refuse to send data to different devices as a result its energy is conserved and its throughput can increase because of self-centered band covering. Similarly a selfish node may modify the medium access control behaviors of the cognitive radio nodes. This attack can also decrease the throughput of the CRN drastically.

2.2.2.4 Defense method for CCSD and SCN

These attacks can be alleviated by using a trust approach allowing each cognitive radio node to be supervised and surveyed by its neighborhood nodes. The neighbors then analyze the observed data and finally determine whether the node is mischievous or not.

2.2.3   Network layer Attacks

Network Layer is responsible for forwarding of packets from sender device located in one network to the receiver device located on a different network. The various problems of security in traditional wireless communications can also be found in cognitive radio networks because of the 3 shared architectures of infrastructure, Adhoc and mesh. CRNs are also similar to WSNs including multi-hop routing protocols and power constraints [26]. Frequent spectrum hand-off due to appearance of primary system makes routing more complex in CRN. The various attacks that target network layer and their defense methods are as follows and shown in table 2.3:

2.2.3.1 Sinkhole Attacks

Sinkhole attacker deceives other nodes that it is the perfect path towards a particular destination thus inviting them to forward the packets through it [36]. Here the intruder is also able to alter or drop the packets from various devices within the network such process is known as selective forwarding. This type of outbreak is more powerful in mesh and infrastructure architectures as all the packets first travel to the base station which permits the intruder to dictate that it is the most appropriate path for passing the packets through the network.

• Defense Methods: This type of attack is difficult to detect. Geographic routing [36] protocols develop a topology on demand using only interactions done locally and data without the help of base station. As a result data will be passed to the base station and will not go anywhere else to produce a sinkhole.

2.2.3.2 Hello flood Attacks

Here the intruder broadcasts the message to all the CR nodes of the network with sufficient power that it is in the neighborhood of them [36]. For instance the intruder may send the packet to the nodes informing them that it is their neighbor and should be used for transmitting the packets to the specific nodes as a result even the far off nodes will use this node for transmitting their packets to specific destination. But these packets may be lost, also if the node suspects the outbreak it cannot send the packets because other nodes may also use the same intruder node to transfer the packets.

• Defense Method: To alleviate this attack a symmetric key is shared between a node and the base station behaving as a trusted third party and establishes the session keys between the participating entities to secure their communication. The 2 parties use the session keys to identify one another and authenticate also.

Table 2.3: Network Layer Attacks and Counter Measures

S. No.	Type Of Attack	Counter Measure
1.	Sinkhole Attack	Protocols based on geographic routing
2.	HELLO flood Attack	Algorithm based on symmetric key
3.	Sybil Attack	i) Radio resource Testing Method ii) Resource testing
4.	Wormhole Attack	i) Utilization of Geographic Routing Protocols ii) Packet Leashes: Geographic and temporal

2.2.3.3 Sybil Attack

Sybil attack is a type of attack where the attacker produces a huge number of fictitious identities and acts like geographically different devices [37]. As it is a complex task to keep a database of different identities because of the existence of many small scale networks managed by multiple managers, CRNs are susceptible to these type of attacks. In the CR network where many devices are striving for white bands, a malicious device may produce a number of fictitious identities. Each of the fictitious identity makes a request for the frequency band as a result fairness of spectrum usage is reduced for other legitimate devices [38].

• Defense Methods: The main idea for defending the Sybil attack is to validate each devices identity. Usually there are two methods to validate the identity as direct and indirect validation. In case of direct validation, validation of one device is checked directly by other device and in case of indirect validation devices that are already validated, validate the identity of other devices. In [37] a method resource testing is proposed for direct validation. Resource testing is based on the assumption that the resources of malicious nodes physical entity are limited. The device is validated by measuring the resources and comparing them with the resources of physical node. In [39] proposed a different validation technique for CRNs. The various assumptions for this technique are: Firstly each physical device consists of only one radio and secondly each radio can only transmit or receive data over one channel at any instant. A device then verifies that its neighboring devices are not Sybil attackers by allocating a distinct channel to each and every neighboring devices on which they can broadcast the packets. A channel is then selected randomly by the challenger on which it listens to the packets to determine whether the neighbor to which channel is assigned is an authentic one or not.

2.2.3.4 Wormhole Attack

In wormhole attack, the malicious node receives the packets in one portion of the network and dispatches them over wired or wireless communication link with lower latency than the default ones. The packets are replayed in other portion of the network. This type of attack is carried out by the authentic users mostly few hops away from base-station that they are only one or two hops far through the attacker [26]. Mostly the users in the network may use the adversary for dispatching of messages when the edge of the wormhole is far away from the base-station. As a result messages may be transmitted selectively to the adversary device that are nearer to base-station for additional dispatching or collected for snooping as they are forwarded [26]. The wormhole attack may result in the division of the network if the attackers are correctly placed. This division of network leads to network route discovery which gives extra knowledge to the attackers to be utilized for different types of attacks [26].

• Defense Methods: In [36] proposed to utilize geographic routing protocols to transmit messages within the network. These geographic protocols build a network topology on routing the messages to the base-station which makes it difficult to divert messages to the wormhole. In [40] the authors suggested adopting packet leashes to reveal and mitigate this type of attack. The paper proposed two different types of packet leashes that is geographic and temporal which ensures that the attacker is detected if the packet is moved more than the allowed leashes. Geographic leash makes sure that the destination of the packet is not so far from the transmitter. For this type of leash every device should have the knowledge of their own position and their clocks should also be roughly synchronized. The transmitter appends their position to the packet and the instant the packet was transmitted. The destination device correlates this information with its position and the time instant of receiving the packet. The destination device calculates the upper bound of the radius among the transmitter and itself. On the other hand temporal leash maintains an upper bound on the duration of packet life which limits the longest navigation length of the packet. In temporal leash the clocks should be tightly synchronized. The transmitter appends the instant when the packet was transmitted, to the packet. The destination correlates the time when the packet was received to the time when it was transmitted due to which the destination gets to know whether the packet had traveled too far or not.

2.2.4 Transport layer Attack

The transport layer is responsible for flow control, error control and congestion control. The attack that targets transport layer and its defense method is as under and shown in table 2.4:

Table 2.4: Transport, Application and Cross Layer Attacks and Counter Measures

S. No.	Type Of Attack	Counter Measure
1.	Key Depletion	Counter Cipher mode with block chaining message authentication code protocol (CCMP)
2.	Cognitive Radio Viruses	Inserting a feedback loop into the network
3.	Loin Attack	Cross layer detection method
4.	Jellyfish Attack	i) A mitigation method in which each device examines their neighbors movements ii) A method that uses the broadcast nature of wireless medium for detection and mitigation of these attacks.

2.2.4.1 Key Depletion Attack

The TCP session times in CRN are shorter because of the large round-trip-time and too many retransmissions [41]. This implies that a large number of TCP sessions are initiated. At the start, each TCP session is associated with a cryptographic key in various transport layer protocols like SSL. As more and more session keys are used there is a chance that some keys may be duplicated. This duplication of keys can be exploited by the attacker to breach the basic cipher system [26]. Various protocols like wired equivalent privacy (WEP) protocol and temporal key integrity protocol of IEEE 802.11 are vulnerable to key repetition attacks [26].

• Defense Method: CCMP (counter cipher mode with block chaining message authentication code protocol) is developed to exponentially deplete key duplications [29]. The proposed protocol uses 128 bit keys associated with 48 bit initialization vector. This approach decreases the susceptibility of the network to replay attacks [26].

2.2.5 Application Layer Attacks

Application layer is the last layer of protocol stack and is the nearest to the final user. This layer has the authority to compute the resources that are available, to synchronize the data transmission and recognizing the nodes. Due to additional responsibility of spectrum sensing and learning, Cognitive Radios need larger transmitting power as compared to classical radios. So they are vulnerable to software viruses and malware [26]. Also, the delays that occur at physical and MAC layer because of frequent handoffs, irrelevant re-forwarding of packets and those that occur due to numerous key exchanges results in decrease in quality of service at application layer [26]. The attack that targets application layer and its defense method is as under and shown in table 2.4:

2.2.5.1 Cognitive Radio Virus

Virus is a malicious program that duplicates itself when executed or poisons other programs by making alterations in them [26]. CRNs are susceptible to viruses in the same manner as the other networks. In CRNs these viruses can be destructive because of its self -propagating nature. A cognitive radio affected by the virus can propagate to other neighboring radios an invalid state. The neighbor radio will pass through this invalid state and the radio will falsely learn to adapt to this atmosphere thus influencing the decision of the network.

• Defense Method: In [7] the authors introduced a feedback loop into the network that enables the cognitive radio to perform learning again when invalid information about the environment is propagated. Another technique is to develop method to disqualify learned actions that are expected to defy certain rules.

2.2.6 Cross layer Attacks

Cross-layer attacks are those attacks that target more than one layer of protocol stack which can disrupt the entire cognitive process of spectrum sensing, analysis and decision [26]. Here the attacker may target one layer however the performance of other layer may be degraded. Various cross layer attacks are as follows and shown in table 2.4:

2.2.6.1 Lion Attack

This attack uses the primary user emulation attack to disturb the TCP link [42]. It is a cross layer attack executed at the physical layer and intended at transport layer where masking an authorized transmission forces a cognitive network to execute frequency hopping and thus transmission control protocol performance will be degraded. Whenever the PUE outbreak occurs all unauthorized users of the band will perform frequency handoffs but TCP will not be aware of these handoffs so it will continue to create logical connections and sending packets with no confirmation from the receiver. When the time of TCP segments will be over then TCP will re transmit the packets with large timeout. As a result there will be more delay and packets will be lost.
• Defense Method: To defend this attack a method [43] is used in which transport layer is made conscious about the happenings at the physical layer by sharing of data between physical and transport layer. Due to this the TCP connections will be stopped during the frequency hand off periods and later readjust them according to the newer network circumstances. Cross Layer Detection based mechanism is used to detect the attack. It is a good solution.

2.2.6.2 Jelly-Fish Attack

It is similar to lion attack because both affect the TCP [26]. In case of lion attack deterioration of TCP occurs because of frequent spectrum handoff. While in case of Jellyfish attack the reduction in throughput takes place due to packets arrived out of order, delayed or dropped [26]. It is executed at the network layer and targets the transport layer. The packets received are deliberately rearranged by the attacker. TCP is susceptible to out of order packets because they provoke re-transmissions and deteriorate throughput. Dropping of packets can also deteriorate throughput [26].
• Defense Methods: In [44] the authors presented a mitigation method in which each device examines their neighbors movements. The devices calculate the ratio of dropped packets in a certain time span for its neighbors that drop packets. This ratio is compared with predefined threshold and if it is

more than the threshold then its neighbors that are at one hop distance to the device dismiss it for a certain time span. In [45] a method is proposed that uses the broadcast nature of wireless medium for detection and mitigation of these attacks. Here the attack can be detected by its neighbors when they are set to examine the activities of one another. In this method packet are transmitted with cumulative sequence numbers and ID number. The nodes that are examining the activities of other nodes are able to detect delayed, dropped or out of order packets if any, by its neighbor. If a threshold of this malicious behavior is exceeded the malicious node is penalized and can even be thrown out of the network.

Chapter 3

LITERATURE SURVEY: PUEA AND ITS DETECTION TECHNIQUES

3.1 Primary User Emulation Attack in Cognitive Radio Networks

As described in chapter 2. Primary User Emulation Attack is a physical layer attack. PUE attack is where the attacker changes its frequency of transmission to emulate the signal characteristics of the primary user and makes the secondary users believe that it is the legitimate primary user signal. As a result secondary users perform spectrum handoff. PUE attack can adversely affect the spectrum sensing mechanism and also decreases the availability of channel to the secondary users extremely [46]. The figure 3.1 shows the scenario of primary user emulation attack.Here we have two bands of spectrum Licensed band I and Licensed band II each having six channels $f_1, f_2, f_3, f_4, f_5, f_6$ and $f_7, f_8, f_9, f_{10}, f_{11}, f_{12}$ respectively. First take an example in Licensed band I in which three channels namely f_1, f_3 and f_4 are used by primary system to send the signals to the primary receiver. The remaining f_2, f_5 and f_6 channels are free which are allowed to be used by the secondary users SU_1, SU_2 and SU_3 for communication. But if a PUE attack occurs e.g. EU_2 may disallow the secondary users from using the free channels by emulating the signal transmitted by the primary user in the channel f_2. As a result of PUE attack the secondary users are made to leave the corresponding channel. Now take the example in licensed band II in which

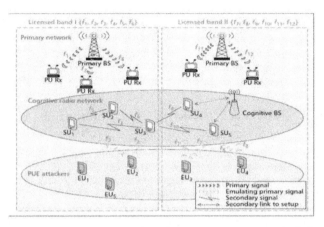

Figure 3.1: Illustration of PUEA in Cognitive Radio Networks [46]

the primary system uses the channels f_{11} and f_{12} and the channels f_9 and f_{10} are used by secondary users SU_4 and SU_5 respectively and the EU_3 and EU_4 attackers mimics the signals of primary users in the channels f_7 and f_8 respectively. Now for example SU_4 and SU_5 requires to search a channel to make connection with the base station but if the attackers EU_3 and EU_4 are not perfectly recognized then SU_4 and SU_5 may not find any channel free and thus they may not be able to make connection with the base station.

3.1.1 Classification of Attackers

PUE attackers are classified as follows:

a. Selfish and Malicious Attackers: The main goal of selfish attacker is to increase its share of spectrum usage [46]. It mimics the incumbent signal making the other unlicensed users believe that the channel is not free and then uses that channel for its own use. On the other hand the goal of malicious user is just to create disturbance in the dynamic spectrum access of secondary users however it does not utilize the channel for its own use.

b. Power-Fixed and Power-Adaptive Attackers: Power-fixed attacker makes use of fixed power that is defined in advance irrespective of the real power of the incumbent signal. On the other hand Power-Adaptive attacker can dynamically alter/change its power for transmission as the transmission power used by primary user signals and channel parameters [46].

c. Static and Mobile Attackers: Static attackers have the location set which
does not vary during the attack. Using various location verification methods
like TOA or TDOA, its position can be obtained. Static attackers are easy
to get detected [46]. Mobile attacker on the other hand changes its location
with time during the course of attack. As the mobile attacker changes its
location it is hard to detect the mobile attacker.

3.1.2 Impact of Primary User Emulation Attack in CRN

Primary User Emulation Attack results in a number of complications in the
cognitive radio networks [46]. Some of the complexities are:
• QoS Deterioration: Primary User Emulation attack adversely affects the
QoS of CRN by spoiling the consistency of secondary services [46]. E.g. PUE
attacker may cause secondary users to vacate the channel frequently by mod-
ifying their operating frequency bands due to which secondary services may
have large delay or jitter.
• Denial of Service: PUE attacker may cause denial of service because the
secondary users may have inadequate frequency bands for communication
and thus the secondary services will be stopped [46]. In some cases the CRN
may not get any channel for common control channel which is for transferring the control messages. As a result cognitive radio system may be halted.
This is known as the Denial of Service.
• Bandwidth Waste: As it is known that the main goal of cognitive radio networks is to utilize the spectrum efficiently but the presence of PUE attackers
may snatch away the white spaces from the legitimate secondary users which
causes the wastage of bandwidth.
• Interference with the Primary Network: PUE attacker can also cause disturbance to the primary system if the PUE attacker is not able to detect the
primary user [46].

3.2 Detection of Primary User Emulation At-
tack in Cognitive Radio Networks

3.2.1 DRT (Distance Ratio Test) & DDT (Distance Difference Test) Method

The author in [16] first describes the Primary User Emulation Attack in
which the attacker transmits the signal that has the same features as that of

Primary User signals. This type of attack adversely affects the CRN because it affects the very first function of CR node that is the sensing of spectrum. In this paper the author next proposes a transmitter verification mechanism (non-iterative method) which uses the location verification method to differentiate between the Primary User signal and the attacker signals. This transmitter verification can be combined with spectrum sensing to improve its truthfulness. Two location verification methods are used for transmitter verification namely Distance Ratio Test (DRT) and Distance Difference Test (DDT). The DRT is based on RSS (Received Signal Strength) values calculated by a pair of location verifiers (LVs) to verify the position of signal source whereas DDT is based on the difference in the phase of primary user signal calculated at a pair of location verifiers (LVs) to authenticate the position of signal source. Two types of location verifiers are used master LVs and slave LVs. Master Location Verifier contains a database of coordinates of each and every Primary TV tower. The results show that the position of attacker in the vicinity of location verifiers can affect the work of both the methods.

3.2.2 Loc-Def (Localization-based Defense) Method

The author in [17] proposed a transmitter verification scheme known as LocDef (localization-based defense). The method determines whether the signal is from the legitimate primary transmitter by calculating its position and analyzing the characteristics of the received signal. This method assumes that the primary transmitters are fixed TV towers and if the source of transmitted signal wander from the predefined position of TV towers and also the features of the signal is similar to those of primary transmitter then it is possible that the signal source is the primary user emulation attacker. Contrastingly the PUE attacker may try to avoid this detection method by transmitting from the nearby region of the TV towers. In this case the characteristics of signal along with the transmitter position are used for revealing the attack. This method has three main parts: Signal characteristic analysis, calculating the energy levels of received signal and locating the transmitter of the signal. Non- Iterative approach is used to detect the attack. The method uses the Wireless Sensor Network to gather the received signal strength (RSS) measurements in the network. Then by detecting the peaks in the RSS measurements location of transmitting source can be determined.

3.2.3   Dogfight in Spectrum

The author in [47] proposed a Dogfight among the PUE attacker and the
secondary users in cognitive radio system with unexplained data about the
channels. A blind game is established between the secondary user which acts
as guardian against the attack and the PUE attacker. An adversarial bandit
algorithm is used to combat the unexplained channel data and inconsistent
policies of the PUE attacker. The secondary user or guardian assumes every
band as a bandit arm and applies a method of adversarial multi-armed bandit
as its policy. This paper has examined various types of PUE attacker policies
like uniformly random, selectively random and maximal interception. Also
the cases of full and half information about various channels are examined.
Simulation results show that the decrease in performance reduces with the
rising temperature.

3.2.4   Hearing is Believing: Detecting Mobile PUEA in White Spaces

The author in [48] proposed a technique to reveal the attacker of mobile PUs
known as Hearing is Believing. In this method every SU is embedded with an
acoustic sensor. For revealing the mobile attacker a disabling beacon protocol
is applied in which a specifically produced signal is sent prior to initiating
the microphone. By adding extra data like digital signatures with the beacon
secondary users can distinguish among authentic wireless microphones and
PUE attackers. Interrelationships between the radio frequency signal and the
acoustic data collected by the sensor are used to distinguish between the PUE
attackers and legitimate wireless microphones. On evaluating the proposed
technique it is seen the technique can acquire false negative and false positive
rates of less than 0.1 in just 3 seconds and also the time required for detection
can be decreased more if recovery white-space machines are accessible.

3.2.5   Belief Propagation Method

The author in [49] proposed a defending mechanism to counter the primary
user emulation attack in cognitive radio networks by applying a belief propagation method. In this method each secondary user performs some computations for local functions and the compatibility function and also calculates
the messages and interchanges them with the adjacent users in an iterative
manner using belief propagation. When BP converges the attacker will be
revealed based on the mean of all the final beliefs. The attacker is revealed
by comparing the mean of final belief with the predefined threshold if mean is

lower than threshold then the transmitter is the primary user emulator otherwise the transmitter is the legitimate primary user. When the detection is complete all the secondary users in the network will be informed about the attack, if present and then the secondary users ignore the primary signals sent by the attacker. The main advantage of this technique is that it converges quickly and does not require the use of costly hardware.

3.2.6 TDOA (Time Difference of Arrival) Method

The author in [50] proposed a detection method based on TDOA values and uses Taylor-series computations for optimization of the error that occurs while calculating the position of the transmitter of the signal. This paper also measures the goodness of the proposed method and also evaluates the accuracy of the method. In this method, TDOA is the discrepancy between TOA (time of arrival) of the signal at two or more cooperating nodes measured using a correlation mechanism. TOA (time of arrival) is used to compute the distance from the user to be located to the reference user by calculating the propagation time of the signal which is obtained by sending a signal to the user to be located and that user quickly responds with another signal. The time passed between sending of signal and receiving the response is utilized to measure the distance among the users. The position of transmitter can be obtained onto a hyperboloid with one measurement of TDOA computed between two nodes. If there is another TDOA value then the position of transmitter can be onto second hyperboloid. However the intersection point between the two hyperboloids presents a curve onto which the position of transmitter can be obtained. But in real scenarios these TDOA values encounter errors due to which the hyperboloid hardly intersects. Thus it becomes an optimization problem to minimize this error. This paper uses the Taylor series estimation for minimizing the error.

3.2.7 COOPON Method

The author in [51] defines the new types of selfish attack in cognitive radio Adhoc networks namely signal fake selfish attack (type 1), signal fake selfish attack in dynamic signal access (type 2) and channel preoccupation selfish attack (type 3) and then presents an effective selfish attack detection mechanism known as COOPON having multiple channel resources by cooperative CR nodes. Here the selfish secondary user will broadcast false news about the channel availability so that it can use them freely. The method known as COOPON will reveal the selfish attack using the cooperation of other neighboring nodes. Every neighboring node interchange the channel availability information both received from and sent to the target node. This information is evaluated by the neighboring nodes by comparing the sum of channels described to be used at present by the target secondary user to the sum of channels described to be used at present by all the neighboring nodes. If there is some difference among the two then the nodes will declare the target node as a selfish attacker. This is a simple method.

3.2.8 Database Assisted Frequency Domain Action Recognition Method

The author in [52] proposed a method for detection depending on the operation of action recognition mechanisms in the frequency realm. In this method first the primary users signal characteristics in the form of vectors are stored in the database. Then the signal characteristic vectors of new users are correlated with the vectors in the database. If there is an entry in the database similar to the observed characteristic vector then the result is checked again using artificial neural network for more analyses by calculating the covariance descriptor. However if there is no similar entry in the database then it concludes that the new user is the Primary User Emulation Attacker. This mechanism operates on deflected signals and evaluates it in frequency realm. This is an efficient mechanism especially when networks have multiple primary users. This method can further be improved either by analyzing the effect of frequency selective multi-path fading on the efficiency of the approach or demonstrating the optimality of the action recognition method for detection of Primary User Emulation Attack.

3.2.9 Signal Activity Pattern Acquisition and Recognition System for PUE Detection

The author in [53] proposed a detection method for primary user emulation detection based on Signal Activity Pattern of the signal. The method first extracts the signal activity pattern using spectrum sensing mechanism e.g. ON and OFF periods of the signal where ON period is the time of busy period for which the source is transferring and OFF period is the free time period among adjacent ON periods. This collected activity pattern of a signal is known a SAP. Then the observed SAP is correlated with the SAPs of Primary Users using a Reconstruction Model. If there is a mismatch (obtained in the form of reconstruction error) between the SAP of Primary User and the collected SAP then the source of the signal is the PUE attacker. The main advantage of this method is that it is applicable to any type of attacker (mobile or static) and does not require any previous information about the position of the Primary User. After analyzing the performance of this method the author concludes that SPARS is an efficient mechanism for revealing both straight and smart intruders.

3.2.10 Two-Level Database-assisted Method

The author in [46] proposed a two-level database-assisted method to reveal the primary user emulation attack. It uses the energy detection and location verification processes for quick detection of attack and also proposed mitigation method based on admission control. In this technique a local database is mounted on each secondary node to hold the local sensing data and a global database is mounted on the base station (BS) of cognitive radio network to gather all the local sensing information and also holds the global decisions. So in this method each CR node has 4 main parts: signal preprocessing unit, energy detector, a location verifier and a local database. First the signal preprocessing unit on receiving the signal performs sampling, squaring and aggregation and then the sampled energy vector and aggregated energy is generated by the preprocessing unit. The aggregated energy is passed on to the energy detector to compare it with the predefined threshold. If the energy detector either detects no signal or detects the presence of primary user emulation attacker signal the mechanism is stopped and outcome is decided accordingly. Contrastingly the energy vector is passed on to the location verifier which calculates the position of the transmitter with the Bayesian hypothesis testing and the calculated position are then transmitted to the Base Station for data gathering. The admission control mitigation method is also proposed to mitigate the PUE attack by preserving some part of the channels for spectrum handoff as a result the performance degradation due to PUE attack is decreased.

3.3 Outcome of Literature Survey

From the literature survey it is clear that a lot of research has been done for developing the detection techniques for Primary User Emulation Attack in cognitive radio networks. Various localization techniques have been proposed by different authors and each has their advantages and disadvantages. From literature survey it is clear that wireless location methods fall into two main categories that are mobile based and network based. In case of mobile based location systems, mobile device determines its location by the signals received from base-station or from global positioning system (GPS) while as the network based depends on the measures of certain distance-dependent parameters (e.g. Received signal strength (RSS), Angle of Arrival (AOA), Time of Arrival (TOA)) evaluated at base-station. Primary user emulation attack detection based on localization was considered in [15], [17] [50]. In [17] the author used a localization defense method which introduces both location and signal characteristics of the signal transmitter to verify the primary user signal. The localization process is based on received signal strength (RSS) measurements collected by secondary users and its peak is identified by which its location can be obtained. The decision about the presence or absence of an attacker is done by comparing the calculated location with the known location of the TV tower. This technique is efficient only when the network is small however if the network size increases, the error also increases. This technique has some drawbacks as: Its range is up to only 2 km. Thus, RSS is not suitable for IEEE 802.22 because here the base-station range is about 100 km and also the number of cooperating users is between from hundreds to thousands which is not possible for anyone to predict. It is also vulnerable to high errors because of indoor and outdoor environments.

The authors in [50] introduced advanced cooperative localization method based on TDOA (time difference of arrival) in which base-station gathers the TDOA values from the cooperative users and applies a Taylors series estimation method to locate the position of the signal source. This technique is applicable to IEEE 802.22 but applying Taylor series estimation has some drawbacks as: It requires a good initial value to obtain good results for the attacker location. Also, the convergence of the algorithm is based on the initial values and accuracy of Taylor series estimation is also not so good.

3.4 Problem Statement

As discussed in section 3.3, the existing cooperative localization technique based on TDOA values for PUE attack detection has some drawbacks. In this thesis, we are trying to overcome those drawbacks by using a different algorithm known as Novel Bat Algorithm for localization of attacker. In this thesis, the primary user emulation attacker is detected on the basis of cooperation among various secondary users in IEEE 802.22 cognitive radio network based on TDOA values. Here each and every cooperative secondary device performs spectrum sensing and transmits its recordings to the base-station. The base-station gathers the recordings and applies a cross correlation technique to obtain TDOA measurements from the collected data. These TDOA values are then used to obtain the location of the signal source which can be either incumbent user or the PUE attacker. Our suggested technique based on Novel Bat Algorithm is applied to minimize the Non-linear least square (NLS) fitness function and the maximum likelihood (ML) fitness function to enhance the accuracy of the estimation, reduce the localization error and reduce the number of cooperative secondary users required to detect the PUE attacker.

Chapter 4

PROPOSED SYSTEM FOR PUEA DETECTION BASED ON TDOA USING NOVEL BAT ALGORITHM

4.1 Time Difference Of Arrival (TDOA)

TDOA is the measure of discrepancy between TOA (time of arrival) of the signal at two or more cooperating nodes measured using a correlation mechanism [50]. TOA (time of arrival) is used to compute the distance from the user to be positioned to the reference user by calculating the propagation time of the signal which is obtained by sending a signal to the user to be located and that user quickly responds with another signal. The time passed between dispatching of signal and retrieving the response is utilized to measure the length of separation among the users. The position of transmitter can be obtained onto a hyperboloid with one measurement of TDOA computed between two nodes. If there is another TDOA value then the position of transmitter can be onto second hyperboloid. However the intersection point between the two hyperboloids presents a curve onto which the position of transmitter can be obtained. But in real scenarios these TDOA values encounter errors due to which the hyperboloid hardly intersects. Thus it becomes an optimization problem to minimize this error. There are numerous optimization algorithms that we can use to minimize the error of estimation. In this thesis we are using Novel Bat Algorithm (NBA) for optimization of the Non-linear least square cost function and maximum likelihood cost function and then a comparison is made between NBA and PSO and another between NBA and Taylor series estimation. In addition to this we are also comparing the performance of Grey Wolf Optimizer with the Particle Swarm Optimization. After evaluation, simulation results demonstrates that NBA results in reduced estimation error as compared to Taylor Series Estimation (TSE) and Particle Swarm Optimization (PSO) and Grey Wolf Optimizer also shows reduced estimation error as compared to Particle Swarm Optimization. Both NBA and GWO require lesser number of secondary users for cooperation. Also maximum likelihood function performs better than non-linear least square function.

4.2 System Model for Collaborative Localization Of Primary User Emulation Attacker

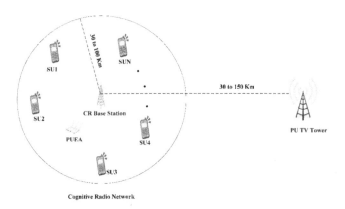

Figure 4.1: System Model

The assumptions used in the collaborative localization of PUE attacker are the following [50]:

• The whole arrangement is comprised of incumbent network with TV towers as transmitters and receivers and a cognitive network having secondary users with a base-station. The base-station has the knowledge of genuine locations of the PUs. The secondary users are static with well-known positions.

- The cognitive radio network range is 30 km to 100 km and incumbent resides outside the network at a length of 30 km to 150 km as shown in the figure 4.1 [54].
- The PUEA can be positioned either within the network or outside the network.
- Errors follow normal distribution with zero mean and are analytically independent [50].

Once the position of signal source is obtained using collaborative localization method, it is then compared with the known position of genuine primary user. If there is a mismatch then the signal source is the primary user emulation attacker otherwise it is primary user. When the PUE attacker is located within the network it can be smoothly and accurately revealed but if it is located outside the network and in the vicinity of genuine PU it is difficult to be revealed and can be puzzled with the primary user. The main goal is to minimize the number of secondary users required for localization and reduce the estimation error. Figure 4.2 shows the flowchart for Detection of PUEA.

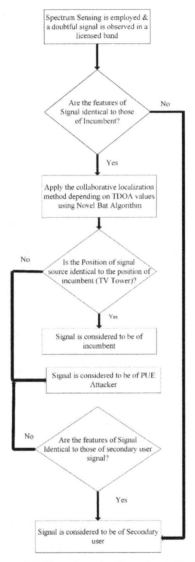

Figure 4.2: Flow chart for Detection of PUEA

4.3 Mathematical Model for Detecting PUE Attacker

Localization of anonymous signal source is a very interesting area of study in numerous fields like military applications [55].Localization method can be classified as mobile based and network based [50] as described in section 3.3 of chapter 3.TDOA makes use of cross correlation technique to obtain the discrimination in the time of arrival of communicated signal at two or more pair of devices. At least three nodes are required to obtain two TDOA values for localization of the signal source as can be seen in figure 4.3. For TDOA measurements tight synchronization is required between the secondary users and base station which is obtained by sending a marker signal from base station to all the secondary users. These secondary users then append this marker signal to their recordings of signals during spectrum sensing at the time instant it received the marker [50]. The secondary nodes then transmit their recording to the base station together with the marker signal which calculates the time passed from when the base station sent the marker to when it is received, thereupon base station is capable of synchronizing the recordings [50]. Now according to the figure 4.1 and 4.3 the system can be defined as: The primary user is a TV tower which is positioned outside the cognitive network at a fixed location. The cognitive radio network has a base-station positioned at origin (x_0, y_0) and N secondary devices that are uniformly distributed over a network area with static locations at (x_i, y_i). The attacker is either positioned within the cognitive radio network or outside the cognitive radio network. The TDOA measurements among the collected

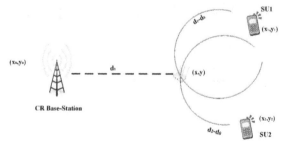

Figure 4.3: TDOA based detection of Attacker

signals at base-station and the ith secondary device [56] can be written as:

$$\tau_i = t_i - t_0 \tag{4.1}$$

Here t_i and t_0 are the time of arrival at secondary user and the base-station, respectively.

If equation (4.1) is multiplied by velocity then a distance equation can be achieved as follows:

$$d_{i,0} = c(t_i - t_0) = c(t_i) = d_i - d_0 \tag{4.2}$$

Here c is the velocity of the signal, d_i is the distance from attacker to i^{th} secondary device and d_0 is the distance from attacker to base-station.

$d_{i,0}$ can be written as [56]:

$$d_{i,0} = \sqrt{(x - x_i)^2 + (y - y_i)^2} - \sqrt{(x - x_0)^2 + (y - y_0)^2} \tag{4.3}$$

The difference in range measurements drawn from TDOA values are written as [57]:

$$r_{TDOA,i} = d_{i,0} + \eta_{TDOA,i} \tag{4.4}$$

Here $\eta_{TDOA,i}$ is the range difference error in $r_{TDOA,i}$. Range difference can also be modeled as follows:

$$r_{TDOA,i} = f(X) + \eta_{TDOA,i} \tag{4.5}$$

Here [57]

$$r_{TDOA} = [r_{TDOA,1}, r_{TDOA,2}, \dots\dots, r_{TDOA,N}]^T \tag{4.6}$$

$$\eta_{TDOA} = [\eta_{TDOA,1}, \eta_{TDOA,2}, \dots\dots, \eta_{TDOA,N}]^T \tag{4.7}$$

$$f_{TDOA}(X) = d_{i,0} = \begin{bmatrix} \sqrt{(x - x_1)^2 + (y - y_1)^2} - \sqrt{(x - x_0)^2 + (y - y_0)^2} \\ \sqrt{(x - x_2)^2 + (y - y_2)^2} - \sqrt{(x - x_0)^2 + (y - y_0)^2} \\ . \\ . \\ . \\ \sqrt{(x - x_N)^2 + (y - y_N)^2} - \sqrt{(x - x_0)^2 + (y - y_0)^2} \end{bmatrix} \tag{4.8}$$

$$X = \begin{bmatrix} X & Y \end{bmatrix}^T$$

In equation (4.5), X is the location of transmitter to be estimated, f_{TDOA} is a non-linear function of X, $\eta_{TDOA}$is the vector representing location error and is assumed to follow a Gaussian distribution with mean 0 and variance $\sigma^2 = \sigma_i^2 + \sigma_0^2$, where σ_0^2 is the base station variance and σ_i^2 is the variance from i^{th} secondary user. However the variance of TDOA is not static value because secondary devices have distinct position. Hence Time difference of arrival is designed as follows:

$$\sigma_i^2 \geq 1 \div 8\pi^2 \times B^2 \times SNR_i \qquad (4.9)$$

Here B is the channel bandwidth, SNR_i is the signal to noise power at i^{th} secondary device [50] which can be written as:

$$SNR_i = SNR_0 - \Delta L_p(dB) \qquad (4.10)$$

Where ΔL_p is the path loss computed from Hata model in suburban areas [50] and SNR_0 is base-station signal to noise power.

$$\Delta L_p(dB) = [44.9 - 6.55(h_p)] \log(d_i/d_0) \qquad (4.11)$$

Where h_p is the antenna height of primary user or primary user emulation attacker

The probability density function for r_{TDOA} is written as [56]:

$$P(r_{TDOA}) = 1 \times \exp(-1/2(r_{TDOA} - d_0)^T) \times C^{-1} \times (r_{TDOA}) - d_0 \div (2 \times \pi)^{L-1/2} \bmod C_{TDOA}^{-1}$$
$$(4.12)$$

Here $C_{TDOA}$is the co-variance matrix for r_{TDOA} values.

Weights W can be calculated based on reliability of each value by taking the reciprocal of variance whose addition can increase the accuracy of localization.

$$C_{TDOA} = W_{ii} = 1 \div \sigma^2 \qquad (4.13)$$

Equation (4.5) represents a number of non-linear equations that needs to be solved. In this thesis we solve them by using Novel Bat Algorithm and Particle Swarm Optimization minimizing the Non-linear least square and Maximum likelihood objective functions to obtain the location of transmitter.

4.3.1   Taylor- Series Estimation

Equation (4.5) is solved using Taylor-series estimation to locate the attacker. Once a series of TDOA values have been obtained r is calculated, then the base-station begins an iterative method with a starting guess of (x_v, y_v) which is renewed at each iteration as $x_v + \delta_x, y_v + \delta_y$ by calculating the local non-linear square error correction (δ_x, δ_y) . The error can be indicated in matrix form as [54] [58]:

$$e = \begin{bmatrix} r_{TDOA} - f_{TDOA,1}(X) \\ r_{TDOA} - f_{TDOA,2}(X) \\ \cdot \\ \cdot \\ \cdot \\ r_{TDOA} - f_{TDOA,N}(X) \end{bmatrix} \tag{4.14}$$

The error function is given by [54]:

$$e_{nonlinear} = r - f(\tilde{X}) \tag{4.15}$$

Where $\tilde{X} = \begin{bmatrix} \tilde{x} & \tilde{y} \end{bmatrix}^T$ is the optimization variable for x.
The linear form of distance error is given as follows [57]:

$$\hat{e} = A\delta + e \tag{4.16}$$

Where

$$e = \begin{bmatrix} \hat{e_1} \\ \hat{e_2} \\ \cdot \\ \cdot \\ \cdot \\ \hat{e_N} \end{bmatrix}$$

$$\delta = \begin{pmatrix} \delta_x \\ \delta_y \end{pmatrix}$$

$$A = \begin{bmatrix} a_{1x} & a_{1y} \\ a_{2x} & a_{2y} \\ \cdot & \cdot \\ \cdot & \cdot \\ \cdot & \cdot \\ a_{Nx} & a_{Ny} \end{bmatrix}$$

$$a_{ix} = \delta e_i(x, y) \div \delta x \mid_{x=x_p}$$
$$a_{iy} = \delta e_i(x, y) \div \delta y \mid_{y=y_p}$$

Value of δ, that minimizes the weighted sum of errors can be evaluated as [57]:

$$\delta = -[A^T A]^{-1} A^T e \tag{4.17}$$

By applying weights δ can be reported as:

$$\delta = -[A^T A]^{-1} A^T W e \tag{4.18}$$

As a result initial guess is renewed as:
$$x_v^i = x_v + \delta_x$$
$$y_v^i = y_v + \delta_y$$

4.3.2 Non-Linear Least Square

In non-linear least square, equation (4.5) is transformed into minimization problem by [56] [58] as:

$$\hat{X} = argmin J_{NLS,TDOA}(\tilde{X}) \tag{4.19}$$

The output of the above equation is the attacker location, and here $J_{NLS,TDOA}(X)$ is the objective function and can be represented as under [54]:

$$J_{NLS,TDOA}(\tilde{X}) = \sum_{1}^{N}(r_{TDOA,i} - \sqrt{(x - x_i)^2 + (y - y_i)^2} - \sqrt{(x - x_0)^2 + (y - y_0)^2})$$

$$= (r_{TDOA} - f_{TDOA})^T \times (r_{TDOA} - f_{TDOA}) \tag{4.20}$$

4.3.3 Maximum Likelyhood

Maximum Likelyhood maximizes the probability distribution function of TDOA defined by equation (4.12) to extract the location of transmitter. Maximum Likelyhood is the weighted version of NLS defined by the equation under [54]:

$$J_{NLS,TDOA}(\tilde{X}) = (r_{TDOA} - f_{TDOA})^T \times W \times (r_{TDOA} - f_{TDOA}) \tag{4.21}$$

And location estimation of maximum likelihood is written as:

$$\hat{X} = argmin J_{NLS,TDOA}(\tilde{X}) \tag{4.22}$$

4.4 Novel Bat Algorithm

NBA is one of the efficient optimization algorithms which can be used to minimize equations (4.20) and (4.21). Bat Algorithm first developed by Yang in 2010 [59] is a Meta heuristic optimization algorithm motivated from the echolocation feature of Bats with changing pulse rates of emission and loudness. To improve the performance of Bat algorithm further, a Novel Bat Algorithm was proposed in [60] by integrating the Bats habitat choices and their self-adaptive allowance for Doppler Effect in echoes in the fundamental Bat. Doppler Effect is defined as the modification in frequency of periodic event when a viewer steps forward in relation to its source.

There are five rules on which NBA is based:

1. Each and every Bat has the information about the discrepancy between the food and prey and environmental obstacles in some way and makes use of echolocation to determine the distance.

2. All Bats fly with velocity v_i at location x_i with frequency f_{min} with changing loudness A_0 and frequency. The Bats can naturally modify the frequency of pulses that are emitted and also modify the rate of pulse emission based on their target.

3. Loudness may change in various ways say from max A_0 to a minimum A_{min}.

4. Each Bat can reproduce in distant habitats based on speculative choice.

5. Each Bat can compensate for Doppler Effect in echoes.

All the N Bats denoted by their position $x_{i,j}^t$ where $i(1, 2, ..N)$ and $j(1, 2, .D)$ and with velocities $v_{i,j}^t$ at time t, begins to find food in D-dimensional search space.

Here NBA is used to locate the Primary User Emulation Attacker by using the echolocation feature of Bats and solve the fitness function given by equation (4.20) and (4.21) for each individual Bat. New solutions are generated as follows:

$$f_i = f_{min} + (f_{max} - f_{min}) *$$
$$v_i^{t+1} = v_i^t + (x_i^t - x^*) * f_i$$
$$x_i^{t-1} = x_i^t + v_i^{t+1}$$

Generalized Novel Bat Algorithm Steps [59] [60]:

Algorithm : Novel Bat Algorithm

Input: Population, habitat choice, weight, rates for Doppler Effect, frequency with which loudness and pulse rate are modified denoted by P, W, C and G respectively.

While (current-iteration < Max-Itearations)

If (rand (0.1) < P)

Produce new solutions

End if
If (rand (0.1)> P)
Produce Local solution surrounding the best solution
End if
Execute the fitness function for each individual Bat
Modify solutions, pulse rate, and loudness.
Rank the solutions and search the current best g_t.
If (g_t does not progress in G time step)
Restart the loudness A_i and fix pulse rates r_i
End if
t = t+1;
End while
Output: The individual with best fitness function value in the population.

The NBA is repeated until termination condition is reached. The individual
with the best value of fitness function is the calculated location of primary
user emulation attacker which has the minimum distance error.

4.5 Particle Swarm Optimization

Particle Swarm Optimization is a bio-inspired optimization algorithm proposed by Kennedy and Eberhert in 1995 [61]. PSO is encouraged by the
communal feature of bird flocking finding their food. PSO has been widely
used in various optimization problems because of its simplicity and efficiency.
The word particle in PSO means the members of the population with neg-
ligible mass and volume and is manipulated with different velocities and
accelerations to improve its behavior. A particle is denoted by four vectors
in the space i.e. current location, best location so far, best location as per
its neighbor and the velocity. The particle modifies its location in the space
depending on the best location found by particle on its own (p_{best}) and the
best location found by its neighbor (g_{best}). In each iteration, the location of
particle and its velocity is modified as follows:
$X_{k+1}^i = x_k^i + v_{k+1}^i$
$V_{k+1}^i = v_k^i + c_1 r_1 (p_k^i - x_k^i) + c_2 r_2 (p_k^g - x_k^i)$
Here x_k^i is the location of particle, v_k^i is the velocity of the particle, p_k^i is the
best retained location, c_1 and c_2 are the constant parameters, r_1 and r_2 are
random numbers between 0 and 1.
Steps of PSO can be summarized as follows [61]:
1. Begin the swarm by allocating a random location to every particle in
space.

2. Solve the fitness functions given in equation (4.20) and (4.21) for each individual particle.

3. Now correlate each particles fitness value with the p_{best} value if fitness value is fitter than the p_{best} then set the p_{best} equal to fitness value and current location of particle x_i as p_i.

4. After this find the particle with best fitness value which is identified as guest and its location p_g.

5. Modify the location and velocities of each particle in the swarm.

6. Repeat steps 2-5 till termination condition satisfies say good fitness value is obtained.

Here the particle with the best fitness value is the location of primary user emulation attacker with minimum error.

4.6 Grey Wolf Optimizer

Grey Wolf Optimizer proposed in [62] by Seyedali Mirjalili, Seyed Mohammad Mirjalili and Andrew Lewis is a meta-heuristic optimization algorithm encouraged from grey wolves. Grey Wolf Optimizer imitates the leadership hierarchy and hunting techniques from Grey Wolves. Also few important steps namely hunting, seeking for victim, surrounding and attacking the victim are carried out [62].

Grey Wolf is from the Canidae family who desire to live in groups of size 5-12 on an average. The leadership hierarchy of Grey Wolves is shown in Fig.4.4. At the top of hierarchy are the males and females called alphas (α) which are the decision makers of the group like decision about hunting, sleeping etc. Alpha wolves are also known as dominant wolves since their decision are to be followed by all the group members. At the second level the wolf is known as beta (β)wolf. These are the subordinates for alphas that help them in making the decisions for the group [62]. The beta wolf can be male or female and is one of the most suitable wolf incase alpha wolf passes away or becomes old to lead. At the lowest level is the omega (ω) wolf which is dominated by all other wolves. And then there is a delta (δ)wolf which is not the alpha, beta or omega wolf. They need to follow alpha and beta wolves but they can dominate omega wolves. They include elders, hunters, scouts and care takers [62]. In GWO α is treated as the first best solution and β and δ are treated as the 2nd and 3rd best solutions respectively. The left out solutions are considered as ω. GWO algorithm performs optimization using alpha, beta and delta whereas omega follows them.

Algorithm : Grey Wolf Optimizer

Figure 4.4: Leadership Hierarchy of Grey Wolf

Input: Max_Iterations, Population of Wolves X_i (i= 1, 2,.n), A, C , a and t =1

Compute the fitness of each individual using equation (4.20)

X_α, the first finest individual

X_β, the 2nd finest individual

X_δ, the 3rd finest individual

While (t < Max_Iterations)

For i = 1 to size_of Population of wolves

every individual modify the location of the present individual

End for

Modify values of A, C and a

Compute the fitness of all individuals using equation (4.20).

Update $X_\alpha, X_\beta, and X_\delta$

T = t+1

End while

Output: X_α

Here the output of the algorithm i.e. X_α, is the estimated location of the transmitter with minimum localization error.

Chapter 5

SIMULATION RESULTS

5.1 Simulation Results

This chapter of the thesis deals with the comprehensive performance evaluation of various algorithms employed against PUEA in CRN. In order to analyze the performance of these algorithms, MATLAB 2015a tool is used. Performance is evaluated in the form of cumulative distributive function and mean error. The area for simulation is taken as 30km*30km with 100 secondary users distributed uniformly in the area and base-station at the origin. The attacker can be positioned either within CRN or outside CRN as shown in figure 4.1. The program is run for 500 monte-carlo simulations and the results are averaged. The techniques Taylor-Series, PSO and NBA using nonlinear least square and maximum likelihood are evaluated and then a comparison is made between NBA and PSO. Another comparison is made between NBA and Taylor-Series Estimation (TSE).

5.1.1 Performance Evaluation Metric

In this thesis, the performance of the Novel Bat Algorithm, PSO and TSE is evaluated based on cumulative distributive function. CDF of a real valued random variable W or just the distributive function of W, calculated at w, is the probability that W will find a value lesser than or equal to w and is given as :
$F_w(W) = P(W \leq w)$
Here F_w is known as CDF of random variable W and $P(W \leq w)$ is the probability distribution.

Table 5.1: Parameter Values for Simulation

Parameters	Values
Antenna height	1.5m
TV tower location	30km : 100km
Bandwidth	6MHz
Lower bound	[-10000 -10000]
Upper bound	[10000 10000]
Number of Cooperative Secondary Users	10 : 100
PUEA Location within CRN	(7000m,1500m)
PU Location	(50000m, 50000m)
PUEA outside CRN	(45000m, 0m)
Dimension	2

Mean Square Error: Mean error is the excellent factor to evaluate the performance of localization methods. MSE is used to calculate the average of the squares of the fluctuations i.e. the discrepancy in expected and what is evaluated.

Mean error is given as follows:

$ME = E[(\hat{x} - x) + (\hat{y} - y)]$

The different parameters used in the cognitive radio network, PSO and NBA are given in the Table 5.1.

5.1.2   Simulation Results of Taylor-Series Estimation

Figure 5.1 depicts the variation of cumulative distributive function (CDF) vs. Distance Error of Taylor-Series and weighted Taylor-Series when the attacker is within the cognitive radio network at (7000m, 1500m), with $SNR_0 = -10dB$ and number of secondary devices equal to 100. In case of weighted TSE when CDF is equal to 0.9, the error is 10 m and incase of un-weighted, the error is 17 m which clearly indicates weighted TSE is more accurate than un-weighted TSE. Figure 5.2 illustrates the effect of increasing signal to noise ratio on the mean error of attackers position in Taylor-Series Estimation.

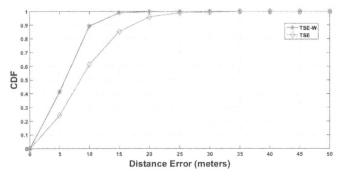

Figure 5.1: CDF vs. Distance error in meters

Here again PUEA is at (7000m, 1500m) and secondary users equal to 10 and 50.It is clear from the graph that as the SNR becomes positive or when the SNR increases, the mean error decreases. Figure 5.3 illustrates effect

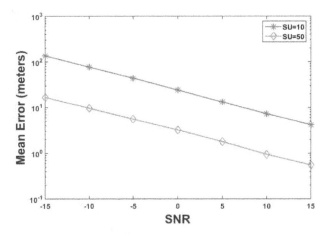

Figure 5.2: Mean Error vs. SNR

of increasing the number of cooperative secondary users on the mean error of attackers position. It shows that mean error decreases with the increase in number of cooperative secondary users in Taylor Series Estimation with PUEA at (7000m, 1500m) and $SNR_0 = -10dB$. Figure 5.4 shows CDF

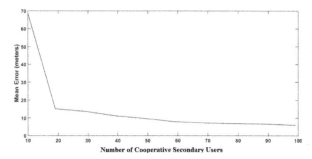

Figure 5.3: Mean vs. no. of cooperative SUs

vs. Distance Error plot when attacker is outside CRN at (45000m, 0m) for Taylor Series Estimation with $SNR_0 = -10dB$ and number of secondary users equal to 100. The graph clearly demonstrates that the mean error is larger when the attacker is outside the cognitive radio network than when it is inside it e.g. at CDF 0.6 error is 100 m. Therefore it is difficult to detect attacker outside CRN rather than inside it.

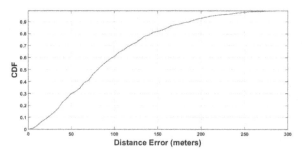

Figure 5.4: CDF vs. Distance Error

5.1.3 Particle Swarm Optimization Simulation Results

For PSO the various parameters used are as follows:

Number of iterations = 200

Population size = 50

Inertia weight = 0.5+ rand ( )/2

$c_1 = c_2 = 1.8$

$SNR_0 = -10dB$

Variation of CDF vs. Distance Error in case of NLS and ML for particle swarm Optimization is depicted in figure 5.5. From figure, it is clear that maximum likely hood function performs better than non-linear least square function for PSO at CDF= 0.7, Distance error for PSO-ML is only 10m however for PSO-NLS error is 15m. Figure 5.6 illustrates Mean Error vs. SNR for particle swarm optimization. It is clear from the figure that with increase in SNR, the mean error decreases.

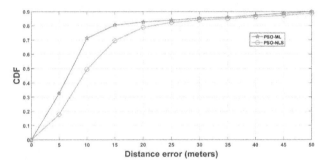

Figure 5.5: CDF vs. Distance Error (meters)

Figure 5.7 demonstrates the variation of CDF vs. Distance Error when attacker is outside CRN at (45000m, 0m) for Particle Swarm Optimization with $SNR_0 = -10dB$ and number of secondary users equal to 100. From the graph it is clear that mean error is larger when the attacker is outside the CRN. For example at CDF= 0.5, distance error is 105m which clearly demonstrates that it is difficult to detect the attacker outside the CRN rather than inside it.

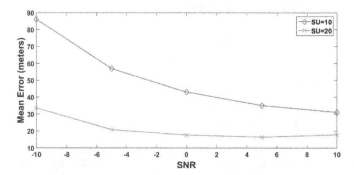

Figure 5.6: Mean Error vs. SNR

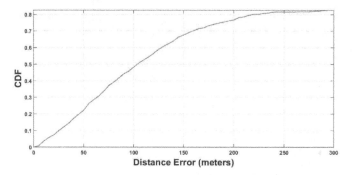

Figure 5.7: CDF vs. Distance Error

5.1.4 Novel Bat Algorithm Simulation Results

For NBA the various parameters used are as follows:

Number of iterations = 70

Population size = 70

G = 30 (frequency of updating the pulse emission rate and loudness)

$SNR_0 = -10dB$

Figure 5.8 depicts the CDF vs. Distance error plots of NLS and ML for Novel Bat Algorithm. From the graph it is clear that maximum likely hood function performs better than non-linear least square function for NBA at CDF equal to 0.4, Distance error for NBA-ML is only 5m however for NBA-NLS mean error is 7.5m. Figure 5.9 illustrates the effect of increasing signal to noise

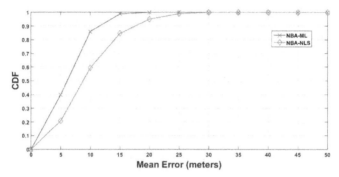

Figure 5.8: CDF vs. Distance Error

ratio on the mean error of attackers position in Novel Bat Algorithm. Here again PUEA is at (7000m, 1500m).It is clear from the graph that as the SNR becomes positive or when it increases the mean error decreases. Figure 5.10

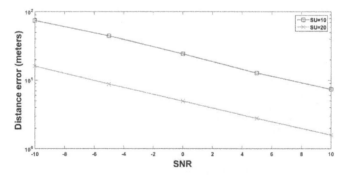

Figure 5.9: Mean Error vs. SNR

depicts the variation of CDF vs. Distance Error when attacker is outside CRN at (45000m, 0m) for Novel Bat Algorithm with $SNR_0 = -10dB$ and number of secondary users equal to 100. From the graph it is clear that mean error is larger in case of attacker outside the CRN than inside it. For example at CDF equal to 0.8, mean error is equal to 150m therefore it is difficult to detect attacker outside CRN rather than inside it.

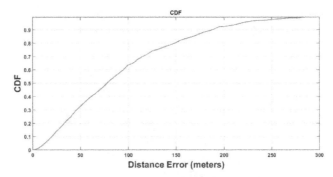

Figure 5.10: CDF vs. Distance Error

5.1.5 Novel Bat Algorithm Vs. Particle Swarm Optimization Simulation Results

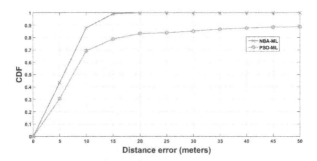

Figure 5.11: CDF vs. Distance Error

Here Novel Bat Algorithm is compared with Particle Swarm Optimization by taking maximum number of iterations equal to 150 and population size equal to 50 for both algorithms.

For NBA, G = 45

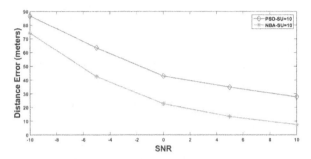

Figure 5.12: Mean Error vs. SNR

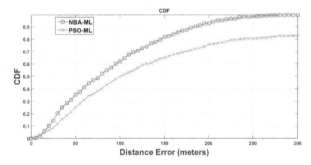

Figure 5.13: CDF vs. Distance Error

For PSO, $c_1 = c_2 = 1.8$ and w $= 0.5 +$ rand() / 2

Figure 5.11 depicts the CDF vs. distance error plots comparing NBA-ML with PSO-ML with PUEA at (7000m,1500m) within the CR network, number of secondary users equal to 100 and $SNR_0 = -10dB$. It is clear from the graph that NBA-ML performs better than PSO-ML. For example At CDF of 0.9 the distance error for NBA-ML is 10 m however for PSO-ML it is more than 50 m. Figure 5.12 illustrates the effect of increasing the signal to noise ratio from -10dB to 10dB with 10 secondary users on the distance error. It is clear form the graph that NBA-ML is more accurate than PSO-ML. It demonstrates that with increase in signal to noise ratio, mean error decreases.For example at SNR= 10dB, mean error for NBA is approximately 8 m however for PSO error is approximately 27 m. Figure 5.13 depicts the variation of CDF vs. distance error, comparing NBA-ML with PSO-ML, with PUEA at (45000m,0m) outside CR network, number of secondary users equal to 100 and $SNR_0 = -10dB$. It is clear from the graph that NBA-ML performs better than PSO-ML and also the distance error is greater in case of PUEA outside CRN than inside CRN. For example at 0.8 CDF, distance error for NBA-ML is 150 m however for PSO-ML error is 225m.

5.1.6   Novel Bat Algorithm Vs. Taylor Series Estimation Simulation Results

Now Novel Bat Algorithm is compared with Taylor Series Estimation. Here PUEA is at (7000m, 1500m) and number of iterations and population size for NBA is 500 and 70 respectively. Figure 5.14 illustrates the plot of CDF vs. distance error. It is clear from the graph that NBA-ML outperforms both TSE and TSE-W. For example at CDF equal to 0.7 distance error is equal to 5m, 7m, 12m for NBA-ML, TSE-W and TSE respectively. Figure 5.15

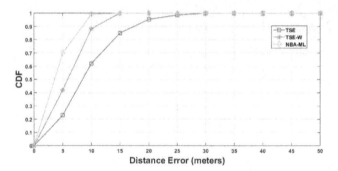

Figure 5.14: CDF vs. Distance Error

illustrates the effect of increasing the signal to noise ratio from -10dB to 10dB with 10 secondary users on the distance error. It is clear form the graph that NBA-ML is more accurate than TSE. It shows that with increase in signal to noise ratio, mean error decreases. The effect of increasing the number of secondary users on the distance error is demonstrated in figure 5.16. In case of NBA, lesser number of secondary users is required for detection mechanism as the error remains constant after further increase in number of secondary users. In contrast to it, more secondary users are required in TSE for reducing the error in detection of PUEA. Thus, NBA outperforms TSE.

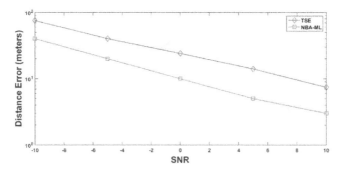

Figure 5.15: Mean Error vs. SNR

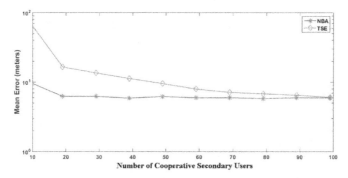

Figure 5.16: Mean Error vs. No. of Cooperative SUs

5.1.7 Grey Wolf Optimizer Vs. Particle Swarm Optimization Simulation Results

Here Grey Wolf Optimizer is compared with Particle Swarm Optimization by taking maximum number of iterations equal to 200 and population size equal to 50 for both algorithms. Also in this case we have taken Primary user emulation attacker at (8000m, 1000m) when within the network and at (50000m, 0m) when located outside the network.

Inertia weight for PSO, w = 0.9

Fig. 5.17 depicts the CDF vs. Distance Error plots for Grey Wolf Optimizer and Particle Swarm Optimization Algorithms using non-linear least square (NLS) as the fitness function with $SNR_0 = -10dB$ and number of secondary users equal to 100. The graph clearly demonstrates that GWO-NLS outperforms PSO-NLS e.g. at CDF= 0.7, the error is 10m and 20 m for GWO and PSO respectively. Fig. 5.18 illustrates the variation of distance error with

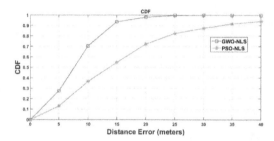

Figure 5.17: CDF vs. Distance Error PUEA inside CRN at (8000m, 1000m)

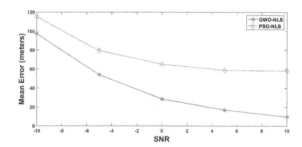

Figure 5.18: Mean Error vs. SNR PUEA at (8000m, 1000m)

the increase in signal to noise ratio with secondary devices equal to 10. It is clear from the graph that GWO-NLS is more accurate than the PSO-NLS. Fig. 5.19 shows the CDF vs. Distance Error plots for Grey Wolf Optimizer and Particle Swarm Optimization algorithms using non-linear least square (NLS) as the fitness function with primary user emulation attacker located outside the CR network at (50000m, 0m), $SNR_0 = -10dB$ and number of secondary users equal to 100. The graph clearly demonstrates that GWO-NLS is more accurate than the PSO-NLS and also the detection of PUEA is difficult when it is located outside the network since it has larger distance

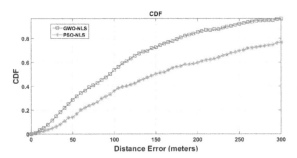

Figure 5.19: CDF vs. Distance Error PUEA outside CRN at (50000m, 0m)

error than when it is located inside it. When CDF = 0.6, the distance error is 110m and 200 m for GWO-NLS and PSO-NLS respectively.

Chapter 6

CONCLUSION AND FUTURE SCOPE

6.1 Conclusion

Cognitive Radio Technology is a developing technology that makes the opportunistic use of white spaces in the licensed band by the unlicensed users without causing any conflict among the licensed users. These networks rely mainly on spectrum sensing to search for white spaces in the licensed spectrum not used by the incumbent users. Malicious nodes can exploit this feature by creating a mirror image of the incumbent signals and cause primary user emulation attack, restricting the secondary users from utilizing the white spaces.

In this thesis we have studied various security threats in CRN and their mitigation techniques. We also have provided brief overview of CRN introduction. We have explained in detail about the primary user emulation attack, its impact on CRN and its various mitigation techniques This thesis solves the problem of Primary User Emulation Attack in CRN using the cooperation among several secondary users based on TDOA measurements and Novel Bat Algorithm where the base-station of CR network is familiar with the position of incumbent in advance. The position of the signal source is estimated and then compared with the known location of the incumbent in order to detect the presence or absence of attack. Two fitness functions which include non-linear least square function and the maximum likelihood function are minimized for solving the various non-linear equations. Simulation results show that this technique is more effective, accurate and better than both Taylor Series Estimation and Particle Swarm Optimization. Also, maximum likelihood performs better than non-linear least square function.

6.2 Future Scope

In this thesis, the technique used is employed for a single attacker scenario leaving the future scope for cases where multiple attacks can be evaluated. The evaluation of multiple attacks using this technique can be taken as a future work.

Chapter 7

PLAGIARISM REPORT

Asia Rehman M.Tech. Dissertation

ORIGINALITY REPORT

%12	%9	%10	%7
SIMILARITY INDEX	INTERNET SOURCES	PUBLICATIONS	STUDENT PAPERS

Bibliography

[1] Beibei Wang and K. J. Ray Liu, "Advances in Cognitive Radio Networks: A Survey," *IEEE Journal of Selected Topics in Signal Processing*,vol. 5, no. 1, February 2011.

[2] Wassim El-Hajj1, Haidar Safa1, Mohsen Guizani, "Survey of Security Issues in Cognitive Radio Networks," *Journal of Internet Technology* Volume 12 ,2011.

[3] Ian F. Akyildiz, Won-Yeol Lee, Mehmet C. Vuran , Shantidev Mohanty, "NeXt generation/dynamic spectrum access/cognitive radio wireless networks: A survey," *Computer Networks. Elsevier*, 2006.

[4] F.K. Jondral, "Software-defined radio-basic and evolution to cognitive radio," *EURASIP Journal on Wireless Communication and Networking*, 2005.

[5] Sazia Parvin , FarookhKhadeerHussain , OmarKhadeerHussain , Song-Han , BimingTian , Elizabeth Chang, "Cognitive radio network security: A survey," *Elsevier Journal Of Networks and Computer Applications*,vol. 35, 2012.

[6] Yenumula B. Reddy, " Security Issues and Threats in Cognitive Radio Networks," *AICT 2013: The Ninth Advanced International Conference on Telecommunications*

[7] T. Charles Clancy, Nathan Goergen, "Security in cognitive radio networks: threats and mitigation," *3rd International Conference on Cognitive Radio Oriented Wireless Networks and Communications*, 2008. Crown Com 2008, 2008, pp 18 (IEEE).

[8] J. Mitola, "Cognitive radio: An integrated agent architecture for software defined radio," *Ph.D. Dissertation, KTH*, 2000.

[9] Mansi Subhedar1 and Gajanan Birajdarok, "Spectrum Sensing Techniques in Cognitive Radio Networks: a survey," *International Journal of Next-Generation Networks (IJNGN)*, vol.3, no.2, june 2011.

[10] Ekram Hossain, Vijay Bhargava , "Cognitive Wireless Communication Networks", *Springer*,(2007)

[11] D. Cabric, A. Tkachenko, and R. Brodersen, "Spectrum sensing measurements of pilot, energy and collaborative detection," *Proceeding of IEEE Military Communication Conf., Washington,D.C., USA*, pp: 1-7,(2006).

[12] Ian F. Akyildiz, Brandon F. Lo, Ravikumar, "Cooperative Spectrum Sensing in Cognitive Radio Networks: A survey," *Physical Communication*, pp: 40-62, 2011.

[13] A. Min, K. Shin, "An optimal sensing framework based on spatial RSS profile in cognitive radio networks," *Proceedings of IEEE SECON*, pp: 1-9, 2009

[14] Rajesh K. Sharma and Danda B. Rawat, "Advances on Security Threats and Countermeasures for Cognitive Radio Networks: A Survey," *IEEE Communications Surveys Tutorials.*

[15] Gaurav Bansal, Md. Jahangir Hossain, Praveen Kaligineedi, Hugues Mercier, Chris Nicola, Umesh Phuyal, Md.Mamunur Rashid, Kapila C. Wavegedara, Ziaul Hasan, Majid Khabbazian, and Vijay K. Bhargava, "Some Research Issues in Cognitive Radio Networks," *IEEE* ,2007.

[16] Ruiliang Chen and Jung-Min Park, "Ensuring Trustworthy Spectrum Sensing in Cognitive Radio Networks," *First IEEE Workshop on Networking Technologies for Software Defined Radio Networks (SDR), Reston, VA*, pp.110-119,September, 2006.

[17] Ruiliang Chen, Jung-Min Park and Jeffrey H. Reed, "Defense against Primary User Emulation Attacks in Cognitive Radio Networks," *IEEE Journal on Selected Areas in Communications*, Vol.26, No.1, pp.25-37, 2008.

[18] Lianfen Huang, Liang Xie, Han Yu, Wumei Wang and Yan Yao, "Anti-PUE Attack Based on Joint Position Verification in Cognitive Radio Networks," *International Conference on Communications and Mobile Computing (CMC)*, Vol.2, Shenzhen, China, April, pp.169-173, 2010.

[19] O. Richard Afolabi, Kiseon Kim and Aftab Ahmad, "On Secure Spectrum Sensing in Cognitive Radio Networks Using Emitters Electromagnetic Signature," *Proceedings of 18th International Conference on Computer Communications and Networks (ICCCN 2009), San Francisco, CA*,pp.1-5, August, 2009

[20] Olga Len, Juan Hernndez-Serrano and Miguel Soriano, "Securing Cognitive Radio Networks," *International Journal of Communication Systems*, Vol.23, No.5,pp.633-652, 2010.

[21] Changlong Chen, Min Song, Chunsheng Xin, Mansoor Alam, "A robust malicious user detection scheme in cooperative spectrum sensing," *Global Communications Conference (GLOBECOM), IEEE*, pp. 48564861,2012.

[22] Qiben Yan, Ming Li, Tingting Jiang, Wenjing Lou, Y. Thomas Hou, "Vulnerability and protection for distributed consensus based spectrum sensing in cognitive radio networks," *Proceedings IEEE INFOCOM*, pp. 900908 (IEEE), 2012,.

[23] Wenyuan Xu, Wade Trappe, Yanyong Zhang and Timothy Wood, "The Feasibility of Launching and Detecting Jamming Attacks in Wireless Networks," *Proceedings of ACM MobiHoc, Urbana, IL*, pp.46-57, May, 2005.

[24] Wenyuan Xu, Timothy Wood, Wade Trappe, Yanyong Zhang, "Channel Surfng and Spatial Retreats: Defenses Against Wireless Denial of Service," *Proceedings of the 3rd ACM Workshop on Wireless Security, Philadelphia, PA*, pp.80-89,January, 2004,.

[25] Saman T. Zargar, Martin B.H, Weiss, Carlos E. Caicedo, James B.D. Joshi, "Security in Dynamic Spectrum Access Systems: A Survey," *University of Pittsburgh, 2011, ¡http://d-scholarship.pitt.edu/2823/¿.*

[26] Deanna Hlavacek, J. Morris Chang, "A layered approach to cognitive radio network security: A survey," *Computer Networks , Elsevier*, 75, 414436, 2014.

[27] Wenkai Wang, Husheng Li, Yan Sun, Zhu Han, "Attack proof collaborative spectrum sensing in cognitive radio networks," *43rd Annual Conference on Information Sciences and Systems CISS,(IEEE)*, pp. 130134,2009.

[28] Chris Karlof and David Wagner, "Secure Routing in Wireless Sensor Networks: Attacks and Countermeasures," *Proceedings of the First IEEE International Workshop on Sensor Network Protocols and Applications, Berkeley, CA*, pp.113-127, May, 2003.

[29] Chetan Mathur and Koduvayur Subbalakshmi, "Security Issues in Cognitive Radio Networks," *Cognitive Networks: Towards Self-Aware Networks, Wiley, New York*, pp.284-293,2007,.

[30] A. Pandharipande et al., "IEEE P802.22 Wireless RANs: Technology Proposal Package for IEEE 802.22," *IEEE 802.22 WG on WRANs*, November, 2005

[31] Ruiliang Chen, Jung-Min Park, Y. Thomas Hou and Jeffrey H. Reed, "Toward Secure Distributed Spectrum Sensing in Cognitive Radio Networks," *IEEE Communications Magazine*, Vol.46, No.4, pp.50-55, 2008,.

[32] Praveen Kaligineedi, Majid Khabbazian and Vijay K. Bhargava, "Secure Cooperative Sensing Techniques for Cognitive Radio Systems," *IEEE International Conference on Communications 2008 (ICC 08), Beijing, China*, p.3406-3410,May, 2008.

[33] Ankit Rawat, Priyank Anand, Hao Chen and Pramod Varshney, "Countering Byzantine Attacks in Cognitive Radio Networks," *IEEE International Conference on Acoustics Speech and Signal Processing (ICASSP), Dallas, TX*,pp.3098-3101,March, 2010,.

[34] Linjun Lu, Soo-Young Chang et al., "Technology Proposal Clarifications for IEEE 802.22 WRAN Systems," *IEEE 802.22 WG on WRANs*, March, 2006.

[35] Joerg Hillenbrand, Timo Weiss and Friedrich K. Jondral, "Calculation of Detection and False Alarm Probabilities in Spectrum Pooling Systems," *IEEE Communication Letters*, Vol.9, No.4, pp.349-351, 2005.

[36] Chris Karlof and David Wagner, "Secure Routing in Wireless Networks: Attacks and Countermeasures," *Ad Hoc Networks*, Vol.1, pp.293-315, 2003.

[37] J.R. Douceur, "The Sybil attack," *Proceedings of 1st International Workshop on Peer to Peer Systems (IPTPS), Springer*, 2002.

[38] Shameek Bhattacharjee, Shamik Sengupta, Mainak Chatterjee, "Vulnerabilities in cognitive radio networks: A survey," *Computer Communications, Elsevier* 36,13871398,2013.

[39] James Newsome, Elaine Shi, Dawn Song, Adrian Perrig, "The Sybil attack in sensor networks: analysis defenses," *Proceedings of the 3rd International Symposium on Information Processing in Sensor Networks, (ACM)*,pp. 259268, 2004.

[40] Y.C. Hu, Adrian Perrig, and David B. Johnson, "Packet leashes: a defense against wormhole attacks in wireless networks," *INFOCOM 2003 Twenty-Second Annual Joint Conference of the IEEE Computer and Communications, IEEE Societies*, vol. 3, pp. 1976-1986, 2003.

[41] H.M. Qusay, D. MAHMOU, "Cognitive Networks: Towards Self-Aware Networks," *Wiley, London*, 2007.

[42] Olga Len, Juan Hernandez-Serrano and Miguel Soriano, "A New Cross-Layer Attack to TCP in Cognitive Radio Networks," *Proceedings of the 2nd International Workshop on Cross Layer Design (IWCLD 09), Palma, Spain*, June, pp.1-5, 2009,.

[43] Juan Hernandez-Serrano, Olga Len and Miguel Soriano, "Modeling the Lion Attack in Cognitive Radio Networks," *EURASIP Journal on Wireless Communications and Networking*, Vol.2011, Article ID 242304, 10 pages, 2011.

[44] Ning Jiang, Kien A.Hua, Danzhou Liu, "A scalable and robust approach to collaboration enforcement in mobile ad hoc networks," *J.Commun.Netw.* 9 (1) (2007) 56.

[45] Fahad Samad, "Securing Wireless Mesh Networks: A Three Dimensional Perspective," *PhD thesis, University bibliothek*, 2011.

[46] Rong Yu, Yan Zhang, Yi Liu, Stein Gjessing and Mohsen Guizani, "Securing Cognitive Radio Networks against Primary User Emulation Attacks," *IEEE Networks*, July/August 2015.

[47] Husheng Li and Zhu Han, "Dogfight in Spectrum: Combating Primary User Emulation Attacks in Cognitive Radio Systems-Part II: Unknown Channel Statistics," *IEEE Transactions on Wireless Communications*, Vol. 10, No. 1, January 2011.

[48] Shaxun Chen, Kai Zeng and Prasant Mohapatra, "Hearing is Believing: Detecting Mobile Primary User Emulation Attack in White Space," *IEEE Conference*, 2011.

[49] Zhou Yuan, Dusit Niyato, Husheng Li, Ju Bin Song, and Zhu, , "Defeating Primary User Emulation Attacks Using Belief Propagation in Cognitive Radio Networks," *IEEE Journal on Selected Areas in Communications*, vol. 30, no. 10, november 2012.

[50] Olga Leon, Juan Hernandez-Serrano, Miguel Soriano, "Cooperative Detection of Primary User Emulation Attacks in CRNs," *Computer Networks, Elsevier,* Vol. 56, pp. 3374-3384, Sep. 2012.

[51] Minho Jo, Longzhe Han, Dohoon Kim and Hoh Peter In, Korea University, "Selfish Attacks and Detection in Cognitive Radio Ad-hoc Networks," *IEEE Networks,* May/June 2013.

[52] Di Pu and Alexander M. Wyglinski, "Primary User Emulation Detection Using Database Assisted Frequency Domain Action Recognition," *IEEE Transactions on Vehicular Technology,* Vol. X, No. Y, April 2014.

[53] ChunSheng Xin and Min Song, "Detection of PUE Attacks in Cognitive Radio Networks Based on Signal Activity Pattern," *IEEE Transactions on Mobile Computing,* Vol. 13, No. 5, May 2014.

[54] Walid R. Ghanem, Mona Shokair and Moawad I. Desouky, "An improved Primary User Emulation Attack Detection in Cognitive Radio Networks Based on Firefly Optimization Algorithm," *33rd National Radio Science Conference (NRSC 2016),* Feb 2225, 2016.

[55] N. Patwari, J .N. Ash, S. Kyperountas and A. O .Hero, "Locating the nodes: cooperative localization in wireless sensor networks," *IEEE signal processing magazine,* vol.22, pp.54-69, Jul. 2007.

[56] H. C. So, "Source localization: Algorithms and analysis," *Handbook of Position Location: Theory, Practice and Advances, Chapter 2, S.A.Zekavat and M.Buehrer, Eds., Wiley-IEEE Press,* 2011.

[57] Guowei Shen, Rudolf Zetik and Reiner S.Thorma, "Performance Comparison of TOA and TDOA Based Location Estimation Algorithms in LOS Environment," *IEEE Proceedings of the 5th Workshop on Positioning, Navigation and Communication,* 2008.

[58] H. Srikanth Kamath, L. M. Schalk, "Primary User Localization Schemes in Cooperative Sensing," *International Journal of Computer Applications,* (0975 8887) Volume 105 - No. 13, November 2014.

[59] Xin-She Yang, "A New Metaheuristic Bat-Inspired Algorithm," *Nature Inspired Cooperative Strategies for Optimization (NISCO 2010) (Eds. J. R. Gonzalez et al.), Studies in Computational Intelligence, Springer Berlin,* 284, 65-74 (2010).

[60] Xian-Bing Meng , X.Z. Gao, Yu Liu, Hengzhen Zhang, "A novel bat algorithm with habitat selection and Doppler effect in echoes for optimization," *Expert Systems with Applications, Elsevier*, 2015.

[61] Binitha S and S Siva Sathya, "A Survey of Bio Inspired Optimization Algorithms," *International Journal of Soft Computing and Engineering (IJSCE)*, ISSN: 2231-2307, Vol. 1, May 2012.

[62] Seyedali Mirjalili, Seyed Mohammad Mirjalili and Andrew Lewis, Grey Wolf Optimizer, *Advances in Engineering Software, Elsevier* 4661, 69 (2014).

www.ingramcontent.com/pod-product-compliance
Lightning Source LLC
La Vergne TN
LVHW092344060326
832902LV00008B/785